Southern Lights

EASIER, LIGHTER, AND BETTER-FOR-YOU RECIPES FROM THE SOUTH

RECIPES AND PHOTOGRAPHS BY LAUREN McDUFFIE

ILLUSTRATIONS BY TIFFORELIE

Gibbs Smith

For Elle and Easton, little lights of mine.

First Edition
27 26 25 24 23   5 4 3 2 1

Text © 2023 Lauren McDuffie
Illustrations © 2023 Tiffany Mitchell
Photographs © 2023 Lauren McDuffie

Published by
Gibbs Smith
P.O. Box 667
Layton, Utah 84041

1.800.835.4993 orders
www.gibbs-smith.com

Designer: Virginia Snow
Art director: Ryan Thomann
Editor: Michelle Branson
Production editor: Sue Collier
Production manager: Felix Gregorio
Printed and bound in China

Gibbs Smith books are printed on either recycled, 100% post-consumer waste, FSC-certified papers or on paper produced from sustainable PEFC-certified forest/controlled wood source. Learn more at www.pefc.org.

Library of Congress Cataloging-in-Publication Data
Names: McDuffie, Lauren, author. | Mitchell, Tiffany, illustrator.
Title: Southern lights : easier, lighter, and better-for-you recipes from the South / recipes
and photographs by Lauren McDuffie ; illustrations by Tiffany Mitchell.
Identifiers: LCCN 2022046881 | ISBN 9781423661474 (hardback) | ISBN 9781423661481 (ebook)
Subjects: LCSH: Cooking, American--Southern style. | BISAC: COOKING /
  Regional & Ethnic / American / Southern States | COOKING / Health & Healing / General | LCGFT: Cookbooks.
Classification: LCC TX715.2.S68 M3332 2023 | DDC
  641.5975--dc23/eng/20221007

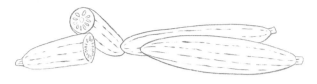

Contents

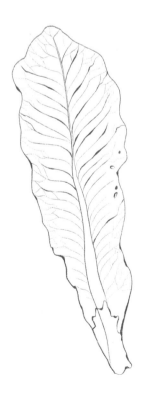

PREFACE

I THINK IT'S WORTH ACKNOWLEDGING, right here at the start of things, that this isn't a book about me. Not really.

From the first page to the last, the entire goal here is to help you go about your days as deliciously as possible while not sacrificing your good health and overall wellness in the process. Or, I suppose we could flip that, and say this book is meant to help you maintain your good health while not sacrificing a bit of deliciousness.

Either way, it is—primarily and above all else—about you. But even so, I do need to talk about myself for just a minute, to provide you with the proper context for it all. *Who even is this person? Why does she call for so much yogurt in her recipes? What does it all mean?*

Admittedly, I have a flair for the dramatic and am prone to verbosity, but I will try to make this short, sweet, and (hopefully) worth your time. I also have a hard-to-shake propensity for punning, and I thank you in advance for your patience with it all. It cannot be helped.

Get to the recipes already!

Y'all—I get it, I really do (that was a food-blogging joke, by the way). I'm excited to get to the recipes myself, but if you'll indulge me for just a moment, I'm going to go about introducing them a little bit . . . *setting the stage*. This is primarily so you'll get a good sense of things, a solid understanding of what it is you are about to read and cook. Just as a movie is drastically more compelling when you know that it is based on a true story, so too is a recipe. Is the backstory going to make the food taste better? Doubtful. But I do believe that understanding the context in which this book lives could very well make it more fun for you to use, maybe more interesting, and hopefully more meaningful.

It is a remarkable feeling to know that strangers are reading your words and absorbing your ideas. But that remarkability evolves into a sort of responsibility when you're asking for not only their time but also their money (ingredients), spaces (kitchens), physical effort (cooking), and occasions. Since I hope to infuse your dinners, lunches, breakfasts, holidays, and all of the occasions in between with these wholesome, Southern-inspired recipes, I have a responsibility to stretch the book at its seams just a little bit, past the recipes themselves, to show you the bigger picture.

My work as a recipe developer and food blogger has provided me the distinct advantage of having this long-running, open-ended dialogue with other home cooks, the people for whom all my work is intended in the first place. As I write and send my recipes out into the world, they are fine-tuned and bettered by the home cooks who give them life in their own kitchens. It's an amazingly educational symbiosis of sorts, this process of working with and for other home cooks, learning what people want and what they don't really dig as much. This has absolutely informed the food you'll see here.

The recipes inside the pages of this book are like living, breathing things that are caught—for now—between two covers. They all have their befores, their unique histories, migrations, and meanderings: their reasons for being. I certainly didn't invent the concepts of cornbread, or savory oatmeal, or snow cream. These are simply things that I love, for one reason or another, and they fit perfectly here. By welcoming them into your kitchen, you, reader, give them new life, releasing them back into the wild . . . continuing and enriching their stories.

And so it goes. From one home cook to another, thanks for that. It's the very best part of it all.

HERE'S THE THING ABOUT SOUTHERN FOOD . . .

SOUTHERN COOKING HAS QUITE THE REPUTATION, doesn't it? *Heavy! Greasy! Unhealthy!* When people heard that I was working on a healthy Southern cookbook, the responses were largely as follows: *Oh, bless her heart. Healthy Southern cooking—that's an oxymoron. There's no such thing!*

Well, with this book, I beg to differ. The scope of the popular narrative surrounding Southern food is, by and large, pretty narrow. It is a cuisine that is well known for its heft and indulgence, its deep-fried items, and its butter-laden fare, particularly outside of the region. While there is obvious validity to this, it's just not the whole story—not even close. As a home cook who has done the majority of her culinary learning in the South, from the foothills of central Appalachia to the sandy, abundant Low Country coastline, I know the whole truth.

We're going to explore and celebrate the broader spectrum of Southern cooking here—both the iconic classics and some lesser-known gems. Though so much of everyday Southern cooking is actually wholesome, incredibly simple, and healthy by all accounts (it's true!), there are still plenty of recipes and occasions where the food adorning a Southern table can be pretty heavy. For many Americans, their exposure to Southern cooking doesn't go much past the popular mainstays (the fried chicken, the biscuits and gravy, the smothered pork chops, etc.). This over-the-top heaviness gives Southern food a sort of infamous charm, and we'll definitely be lightening up some of these classics.

Throughout these pages, I'm going to (politely) refute the claim that Southern food is all bad for you and hopefully breathe new life into some tired, worn-out notions. Once you make your way through the stereotypes, past the overwrought, done-to-death, attention-seeking heavy hitters, the archives of Southern cookery shine with a special sort of brilliance. The great respect paid to all of the goodness that is grown in Southern ground can be felt in so many classic but lesser-known recipes, techniques, and traditions. This truth stands as the guiding force behind much of the recipe selection in this book, as it is very garden driven. We'll shed some light on the quieter chapters of Southern cooking—the healthy, lighter side of the Southern table. It's there, I promise. And it's remarkable, actually. There's a magic to it.

The heart of Southern cooking beats for fresh seasonal produce. There is such great respect for fruits and vegetables, prepared thoughtfully and with no heaviness whatsoever. Much of the Southern diet actually resembles that of the Mediterranean, considered the healthiest in the world. By highlighting some of these truths in simple, straightforward presentations, this book will dismantle the pop-mythologies that brand Southern food as entirely unhealthy, all heavy and guilt-ridden.

Because, you see, that is simply not the case.

HOW THIS BOOK WORKS

THIS IS NOT A DIET BOOK. It's not about losing anything or subtracting this and that. I suppose if we wanted to, we could play a game of recipe limbo. *How low can we really go?* We could whittle these dishes down to mere shadows of their former selves, all for the goal of winning the numbers game. Something like "Name That Tune: Recipe Edition." *I can make a casserole in 300 calories or less, Bob!*

Sure, we could do that. But here's one thing I know for certain: You can serve people the lightest, most low-cal, fat-free food on the planet, but no one's going to eat it if it doesn't taste good. Furthermore, just because something's fat-free or low in calories doesn't mean it's good for you. I'm far more interested in what my food and ingredients do *for* me than what they don't. So we'll politely kick the scarcity mindset to the curb and embrace one of abundance. More is so often more.

The bones of any recipe are made up of ingredients. The magical sorcery otherwise known as everyday home cooking carries us to an infinite number of delicious destinations, depending on the ingredients we select and how we choose to wield them. By picking our ingredients with greater intention and attention, we'll open up a vibrant world of Southern cooking that fully embraces the deep reverence for all of the goodness that is grown in, on top of, and all around the Southern ground.

For the chapters in this book, the notions of health and wellness are guiding lights. From breakfast and lunch to snacks, tea time, and even holidays, this is a decidedly lighter look at the Southern table in its many varied forms. But the crucial companions of taste and flavor are along for the ride as well. These recipes aren't necessarily trying to lure you down the most well-beaten paths of Southern cookery, nor are they attempting to coax you down any roads less traveled. Really, I'd say we're aiming for somewhere in the middle. These are lighter, better-for-you foods built on familiar foundations.

By setting classically heavy recipes to a decidedly more healthful tune and showing off some Southern fare that is light to begin with, I hope to give you ways to enjoy your favorite Southern dishes more often (abundance mindset, remember?). We'll also discover new ways to incorporate classic Southern ingredients and techniques into your cooking repertoire as well (I'm looking at you, pickles). From watermelon, butter beans, and dark leafy greens to buttermilk, honey, and thick, gooey molasses—these pages are bursting with some seriously delicious Southern powerhouses, a true all-star lineup.

I'm not a nutritionist, nor am I a trained dietitian, schooled in the science of food and its nuanced effects on our bodies. But what I am is a cook with a good amount of kitchen common sense—and I bet you've got it, too. Most of us are aware of the basic facts that eating a lot of sugar is not ideal nor is the frequent consumption of deep-fried fare or cooking with calorie-dense saturated fats. These aren't secrets; they're not profound revelations. We all know better.

So the trick, I think, is knowing what to do with this common sense of ours. Rather than ignoring it and making regretful, guilt-ridden decisions, let's invite

common sense to the table. I've got more than a hundred recipes here for you that aim to do just that. This book is filled with big-little ideas and inspiration that are intended to help you (and me) take this common kitchen sense and run with it in the direction of our good health and overall wellness. And run we will, y'all, to some pretty delicious places, if I do say so myself.

SOUTHERN EXCHANGE

THE PRIMARY WAY I WENT ABOUT LIGHTENING UP SOUTHERN DISHES was to simply take a good, hard look at what's in my kitchen—and why. *What fats do I cook with most often, and are there better ones out there that I should be using? Are there leaner cuts of meat that would work just as well in my favorite recipes? Do I really need to be using mayo every single day?*

Looking through a lighter lens, I came up with improvements to my larder (no one I know actually uses this word, but man, I love it). I exchanged some heavier, unhealthy ingredients for more wholesome, lighter ones—things that work with and for my body rather than against it. When I was finished, my kitchen landscape looked so much cleaner, lighter, and more healthful. Furthermore, not a bit of flavor was lost in these efforts. Cool.

Swap Meat

There is certainly a time and place for fatty, rich, succulent cuts of meat. Absolutely. Bacon; sausage; brisket; pork shoulder; skin-on, dark-meat chicken; ribs and rib-eyes. It's all delicious, but not necessarily the type of food we should be consuming all of the time. As such, this book contains lighter, leaner swaps for the aforementioned proteins. We'll just put them to work in different, more thoughtful ways to ensure we get the best flavors and textures possible.

We'll reach for chicken sausage instead of beef or pork. Leaner slices of prosciutto or salty country ham will replace bacon. Juicy, flavorful pork tenderloin will be seasoned just like breakfast sausage, and in one particularly cheeky instance, we'll "pull" strands of tangled spaghetti squash through a homemade BBQ sauce, mimicking the briar patch of fatty pork that is often smashed between two buns.

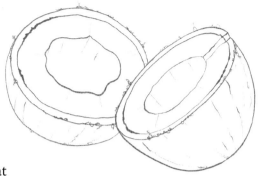

Dairy Bar

There may be no single ingredient more widely associated with Southern cooking than butter. It's like a miracle food, and I love it *beyond*—can you even imagine life without it? I certainly cannot. Same goes for silky full-fat whipping cream, sour cream, cream cheese, and any/all manner of hard and soft cheeses. These things are great. And maybe the best way to preserve and highlight their greatness is to maintain their rarity. If we indulge in them daily, they lose their shine—it's no longer a treat or an indulgence if we do it all the time. I like to treat these cherished, creamy items almost like "special occasion" ingredients. I haven't rid my diet of them entirely; I just don't make a habit of cooking with them every day. They are "sometimes" things.

And so, I'll see your heavy cream and butter and raise you coconut cream and buttermilk.

The items below are *all-the-time things* because they're lighter and more nutritious—they serve us better. As such, they pop up a lot throughout this book's pages. Like, a whole lot.

Buttermilk
Coconut milk and coconut cream
Cottage cheese
Milk
Plain Greek yogurt

Sugar, Sugar

Again, this book is all about *dialing back* on the ingredients that might not serve us best—lightening things up a bit—it's not about turning the volume all the way down. We'll still enjoy sugar, just in different ways and in various forms. We'll use natural, unrefined/less-refined sweeteners like pure maple syrup, honey, coconut sugar, and dates. We'll also watch the portions we use as well, as that is really what it all boils down to, so to speak. While unrefined sugars retain a bit more trace nutrients than the refined stuff, the best rule of thumb is to aim for a reduced intake of sugars all around. So many of the sweets in this book are decidedly less sweet. Which, incidentally, is exactly how I like them. So a win-win there.

Well-Oiled

I could drink olive oil, I really could. In fact, I have. I've done that. It's liquid gold to me, and this book is dripping with it. Sure, there's fat in it—it is an oil, after all. But it's the kind of fat that will go to work for you in such beneficial ways.

So yes, I call for it a lot throughout this book, and most often in its regular state (i.e., *not extra virgin*). People go tit for tat over these things, but for me, it mostly comes down to cost. Extra virgin is pricier, typically, so I like to save it for applications in which it is used more sparingly and its amazing flavor isn't lost—things like finishing raw sauces and salsas, drizzling over finished dishes, and rounding out a great salad dressing.

Unlike some other fats, olive oil has not been linked to weight gain, heart disease, or chronic illness. It is rich in antioxidants and monounsaturated fatty acids and has proven benefits to the heart, brain, joints, and beyond. Plus? It's really delicious.

I call for other cooking fats occasionally, but olive oil is by far the most-used cooking fat in this book, so it absolutely deserves its own preamble here.

LAST LIGHTS

MANY COOKBOOKS HAVE A SECTION LIKE THIS, one where a list of good-to-have kitchen staples is laid out—the last notes and finishing touches that make a dish sing. I always enjoy them because it's like getting a peek inside another cook's kitchen. You learn what's important to them, what they get especially excited about. I've got my own list of worthy pantry essentials for you here, but this one is pared down and tailored specifically to the matter at hand: lighter, better-for-you cooking.

Picture this: You've taken care to prepare a recipe from start to finish and are ready to dig in. You stop to sample your dish and discover that it's just not quite right—something's missing. This is perfectly normal and doesn't necessarily mean that there is anything wrong with the recipe or your execution of it. It just means that it isn't complete yet—it's missing a last, finishing touch.

The proper remedies for lackluster food are usually not *more sugar or more butter!* Rather, they are so often *more acid, more salt, or more crunch!* Like a superhero's tool belt or a magician's bag of tricks (pick a metaphor, any metaphor), each item listed here is something I reach for to give my food that extra je nais se quoi (or "wang," as my grandma would've said). These things fill in the flavor gaps in a big way: They complete the scene—without weighing anything down. Like delicious whispered secrets from me to you, this is my essential list of flavorful, finishing touches.

BUTTERMILK » Another creamy ingredient you'll spot throughout this book is buttermilk. Despite what the name might have you believe, buttermilk doesn't contain any butter whatsoever and is actually a fermented and cultured milk product that contains beneficial bacteria and nutrients. Its distinctly sour taste helps achieve deeper, balanced flavors in so many things, from a Crispy Coleslaw Pancake (page 74) to a Bursting-Berry Company Cake (page 213).

FLAKY SEA SALT » James Beard so famously posed the question, "Where would we be without salt?" Salt is, by far, the ingredient of greatest power and influence in my kitchen. It's the boss. Without it, so many recipes would live in bland, boring states of tragically wasted potential. To build flavor and to achieve adequate seasoning, I keep a small pinch pot of flaky sea salt at the ready, and I use it to finish almost everything that hits my table, from roasted chicken to crispy potatoes. It can take a recipe from mediocre to mouthwatering in a hurry.

FRESH HERBS » There is no shortage of bright green herbs throughout the photos in this book. This isn't just for appearances (though green is my favorite color); it reflects a genuine everyday trick of mine. There are few meals that don't get a shower of verdant, fresh herbs before hitting my table, as it is an amazing way to achieve a burst of freshness, nutrition (hello, watercress), and massive flavor (talking to you now, arugula). Even my desserts often get a bit of chopped mint or basil for the same reasons. Keeping a small-yet-mighty selection of green herbs in the fridge is a great way to finish recipes and bring them to life in such a simple yet impactful way (chef's kiss).

LEMONS » Sprinkle lemon zest over roasted or sautéed vegetables, and stir lemon juice into everything from soups, dips, and sauces to dressings and stews. With its transformative sunshiny brightness, almost everything can benefit from a squeeze of lemon.

SEEDS » Sometimes the crunch of flaky sea salt can be just the thing, and the same can be said for the textural pick-me-up of seeds. Yes, seeds! From dressings to side dishes and even the main event, showering seeds in every color of the rainbow over finished dishes adds this addicting micro-crunch that you really can't get anywhere else. Black and toasted sesame seeds, Charleston's beloved benne seeds, mustard seeds, fennel seeds, celery seeds, and even pumpkin and pomegranate seeds are all things I use on the regular. It sounds pretentious to say that I'm always looking to *increase the textural interest* in my dishes. But it's accurate all the same. I'm just here living out my truth, one poppy seed at a time.

SPICE » Sometimes the thing that's keeping a dish from achieving greatness is a noticeable lack of spice. So many recipes are improved by just a hint of heat, whether from simple cracked black pepper, a sprinkling of pickled jalapeños, or a splash of tasty hot sauce. The Chicken Fricassee (page 170) in this book, for example, is made all the better by a finishing drizzle of hot sauce, and the same goes for the Tuna Salad with Roasted Lemon, Crunchy Potatoes, and Green Beans (page 67) and Jezebel Chicken (page 177). The flavors in these dishes might be perfect for you, just as they are. But if not, try a dash of something spicy and see what that does for you. Hot sauce, pickled jalapeños, crushed red pepper, chipotle powder, and hot paprika are my A-team.

STOCK CONCENTRATES » I use vegetarian, chicken, and/or beef stock concentrates not to make stock itself but to add quick, deep flavor to my soups, stews, dressings, and sauces. A little goes a long way, which is a key trait in some of my favorite lighter cooking staples. You don't need much to make your food sing.

SWEETNESS » I keep a few nice bottles and jars of honey and pure maple syrup close by at all times when I'm cooking, and I can't tell you how often I reach for them, seeking a little burst of natural sweetness in this and that. The almost smoky-sweet flavor of good-quality maple syrup is amazing when drizzled over fall soups like my Two-Ingredient Squash and Caramelized Onion Soup (page 188), and of course, it's the champion of any breakfast table. Honey brings its special floral sweetness to any recipe, balancing out a spicy Scorned-Women Hot Sauce (page 24) or politely sweetening Grits and Honey Granola Bars (page 116).

TOASTED NUTS » Just as tiny seeds are wonderful for adding texture to our dishes, so too are toasted nuts. But they also happen to bring a ton of flavor to anything lucky enough to be topped with them. Toasting nuts only takes a few minutes and the flavor difference is huge—it's absolutely worth doing. All varieties are welcome here, as my kitchen is basically an equal opportunity employer when it comes to nuts. As a Virginia-raised girl, I have a special affection for peanuts, but pistachios, pecans, and walnuts are also interchangeably delicious. The almost browned butter-like flavor of toasted hazelnuts around the winter holidays is one of the very best things, I think.

To toast nuts: Put them on a rimmed baking sheet and roast in a 350°F oven until fragrant and golden brown, 6 to 10 minutes, depending on the nut.

VINEGARS » Speaking of mediocrity, another tried-and-true cure so often can be found in the uplifting perkiness of vinegar. Like a fast and furious breath of fresh air, a simple splash of vinegar transforms so many things from "just okay" to "absolutely delicious." Similar to the buoyancy offered by lemon juice, vinegar can take things even further with its bold assertiveness and strong acidic bite. My go-to vinegars are apple cider and balsamic, but there is a whole wide world of them out there, and experimentation and exploration are fully encouraged.

YOGURT » I've made a very conspicuous switch to Greek yogurt in my kitchen, as a more nutritious substitute for butter, mayonnaise, sour cream, and cream cheese. It is not only a healthier option, but it's also incredibly flavorful and works beautifully as a rich and creamy element in salad dressings, dips, drizzles, and even desserts. Many of the recipes in this book have yogurt going on somewhere, and they're all the better for it.

FRIDGE DOOR THINGS

These are the extras. Inspired by some of my favorite Southern flavors, these are the special homemade mixes and blends of this and that to keep around when your food needs a quick boost. Everything here is designed to really grow the flavors in the foods we cook, without weighing them down. One of my best tricks for sustainable, satisfying light cooking is to lean into this category of "fixin's." These are the crunchy-creamy-salty-herby-spicy-addictive add-ons that can quickly elevate an otherwise ordinary dish into something very special.

I don't have all of these things around all of the time (let's be honest). But on any given day, if you were to poke around in my kitchen, you'd likely spot several of these items ready and waiting to give a seriously delicious kick to my simple everyday cooking. From an all-purpose sauce that goes well on just about anything to the sweet-salty-spicy-tangy salad dressing that hits all the right notes, this collection is filled with flavorful pinch hitters that will far surpass anything you can find on a store shelf.

Southern Summer Concentrate

This concentrate is meant to capture the best flavors of a summer garden, frozen in time (or ice cube trays), so you can infuse your soups, stews, and sauces with that goodness all year long. Imagine the most potent, intense vegetable stock you've ever had, with the addition of fruit and floral components as well: figs, tomatoes, edible wildflowers (if you're feeling fancy), peaches, alliums, and fresh vegetables. Please do reach for the things that sound best to you; use my recipe here as more of a loose guide. Want a little spice? Half of a seeded jalapeño would be great here. Feeling poetic? A squeeze of fresh lemon juice would be a fine nod to summer sunshine.

Makes about 1¼ cups

3 tablespoons olive oil
2 large carrots, chopped
2 celery stalks, chopped
1 Vidalia onion or a comparably sweet onion, chopped
1 small to medium zucchini or yellow squash, chopped
1 garlic clove, smashed
3 fresh or dried figs or 2 pitted dates, chopped
1 peach, peeled and roughly chopped
2 Roma tomatoes, quartered
1½ teaspoons salt
¼ cup water
2 tablespoons chopped fresh dill
¼ cup chopped fresh basil
¼ cup edible wildflowers (optional)

In a large pot over medium heat, heat the oil. When it's hot, add the chopped carrots, celery, onion, zucchini, garlic, figs, peach, tomatoes, and salt. Cook, stirring frequently, for 10 minutes. Add the water and cook for 6 to 8 minutes more or until the veggies are very tender.

Transfer the mixture to a blender. Add the dill, basil, and edible flowers (if using), and blend until it's as smooth as you can get it. You can pour in a little more water to get things moving, if needed.

Pour the mixture back into the pot over medium-low heat, and stirring occasionally, simmer gently to reduce the excess moisture (i.e., concentrating it). This should take about 45 minutes.

To store your concentrate, let the mixture cool to room temperature and (this is what I do) divide it evenly among ice cube trays. Cover the trays in plastic wrap or put them in large resealable bags. This way, you can pop out cubes of concentrate when you need them, ready to melt into your soups, stews, and sauces. They will keep in the freezer for up to 5 months.

Herby, Lemony Yogurt

Resembling a healthier version of green goddess dressing, this one is best pals with all manner of vegetables and is especially great under a heap of Honey-Roasted Radishes (page 131). It is intended to be more of a baseline template than any stone-set thing, so use the aromatics and greenery that you like (try adding garlic), and the amounts of each that feel right.

Makes 1 cup

1 cup plain Greek yogurt
3 tablespoons chopped fresh mixed herbs (I like chives, basil, dill, and cilantro)
Zest of 1 lemon, and the juice of half of it
¼ teaspoon nutritional yeast
2 teaspoons olive oil
1 teaspoon salt
Lots of freshly ground black pepper

Combine the yogurt, herbs, lemon zest and juice, nutritional yeast, oil, salt, and pepper in a bowl and whisk until everything is very well mixed. Adjust the ingredients until the taste and consistency are to your liking (more oil makes it very salad dressing-esque). Keep covered in the refrigerator for up to 1 week.

Yogurty Whipped Cream

Half of the volume of this fluffy, cloudlike dream-whip is made up of healthy yogurt. So yes, it is a great excuse to pile more whipped cream onto any and every thing, if you were wondering. Permission granted.

Makes about 2 ½ cups

1 tablespoon honey, plus more to taste
1 cup vanilla Greek or regular yogurt
1 cup heavy whipping cream

In a medium bowl, combine the honey and yogurt.

Pour the cream into a mixing bowl or into the bowl of a stand mixer fitted with the whisk attachment. Beat on medium speed for 2 to 3 minutes, until soft peaks form. Add the honeyed yogurt and whip on high speed until stiff peaks form, another 2 to 3 minutes. Taste and add more honey if you like things a little sweeter—it's up to you!

This is more shelf-stable than regular whipped cream and should keep nicely in the fridge for a couple of days.

Comeback Sauce

Hailing from Mississippi, this is a great sauce for sandwiches and wraps, and I love it with roasted vegetables. I use both powdered and fresh garlic for a deeper flavor, and my lightened-up version is free of both oil and sugar. Built on pantry staples, this sauce was named in honor of the classic Southern send-off, "Y'all come back now, you hear?"

Makes 1 ½ cups

¾ cup plain Greek or regular yogurt
3 tablespoons chili sauce or ketchup
1 teaspoon spicy brown mustard
2 tablespoons hot sauce or spicy pickle juice

2 teaspoons Worcestershire sauce
1 teaspoon freshly ground black pepper
½ teaspoon garlic powder
1 teaspoon minced fresh garlic

In a medium bowl, combine the yogurt, chili sauce, mustard, hot sauce, Worcestershire sauce, black pepper, garlic powder, and garlic, stirring until nicely blended. This will keep in a covered container in the refrigerator for up to 2 weeks.

Tahini, Cardamom, and Date Caramel

A game-changer of a recipe, date caramel is truly amazing stuff. I slather it on pretty much anything I can from Apples with Smoked Almonds (page 204) to thick slabs of Boozy Bananas Foster Bread Pudding (page 205).

Makes about 1 ½ cups

1 ½ cups pitted dates
⅓ cup vanilla almond milk
2 tablespoons maple syrup
1 teaspoon coconut sugar

1 teaspoon vanilla extract
¼ teaspoon ground cardamom
2 teaspoons tahini
Pinch salt

In a medium bowl, cover the dates with boiling water and let sit for 10 minutes to soften. Reserve a couple of tablespoons of the liquid before draining.

Transfer the drained dates and the reserved liquid to a blender, along with the almond milk, maple syrup, coconut sugar, vanilla, cardamom, tahini, and salt to taste. Blend fast and furiously until the mixture is totally smooth. Transfer to a cute serving dish. Alternatively, you can store this in a covered container in the fridge for up to 2 weeks.

Caramelized Onion and Pimiento Slather

I love dips! Love them. This one especially. It really is here to show that pimientos, what with their fruity sweetness, can make an amazing dip without the help of cheese or mayonnaise. This stuff makes the best toast. It's also killer on a grazing board. Top with some roasted mushrooms and/or an egg and a little spicy arugula, and you've got one of my favorite lunches. It's also great stirred and blended into soups and stews as it offers an extra plant-based burst of flavor. I always use sweet Vidalia onions when I can get them, but a comparably sweet variety will work just fine.

Makes about 1½ cups

2 teaspoons olive oil
2 sweet onions, sliced
Water

1 (4-ounce) jar diced
   pimientos, drained
¾ teaspoon salt

Put the oil in a skillet set over medium heat. When it's hot, add the sliced onions and cook, stirring frequently, for 10 minutes. Add ¼ cup of water and cook, stirring occasionally, until the water has evaporated. Repeat this process (water, stir, evaporate, water, etc.) until the onions have reached a very soft consistency and have a medium-brown, amber color. This process takes about 40 minutes.

Transfer the onion mixture to a food processor and add the pimientos and salt. Blend until smooth, taste for salt, and add more if you think it needs it. This will keep in a covered container in the fridge for up to 1 week.

Scorned-Women Hot Sauce

My dad collected hot sauces when I was growing up, and they always had the most intriguing, tell-me-more names. I've been making my own homemade hot sauces for a while now, but this recipe is actually a marriage between a great store-bought bottle and a totally-from-scratch version. We're going to doctor up a simple bottle of hot sauce into a garlicky, molasses-y concoction that will stop shows and steal scenes. Play around with my template here; make it yours. Give it your own fun name! But if you do, please be sure to let me know what you come up with. That's the only rule.

Makes about 1½ cups

12 garlic cloves
1 teaspoon onion powder
2 teaspoons molasses
3 teaspoons honey
1 canned chipotle pepper in adobo, chopped
1 (12-ounce) bottle hot sauce (such as Frank's RedHot)
Salt

Preheat the oven to 350°F.

Put the garlic on a sheet of aluminum foil and wrap into a little packet. Place this in the oven, directly on the rack, and roast for 35 minutes.

Put the roasted garlic into a blender, add the onion powder, molasses, honey, chipotle pepper, and hot sauce. Blend on high until the sauce is as smooth as you can get it. Taste and season with salt if needed. Transfer to a lidded storage bottle or container. This will keep in the refrigerator for up to 3 weeks.

BBQ Spice Blend

This blend takes its cues from Indian masala chai, my favorite tea. I call for this blend in a few key places throughout this book, but it definitely isn't limited to just those recipes.

Makes about ½ cup but is easily multiplied

2 tablespoons smoked sweet paprika
1 tablespoon ancho chile powder
¼ teaspoon ground cinnamon
2 teaspoons ground cumin
¼ teaspoon ground cloves
½ teaspoon ground cardamom
1 tablespoon lemon pepper
1 teaspoon garlic salt

In a lidded container, combine the paprika, chile powder, cinnamon, cumin, cloves, cardamom, lemon pepper, and garlic salt and shake well. Store in a cool, dry place for up to 3 months.

Note *A big bowl of juicy melon and ripe peaches covered in this spice blend is basically the best fruit recipe I could share. It doesn't need to be any fussier or fancier than that.*

My Favorite BBQ Sauce

You're right. Miso isn't Southern. The incredibly flavorful, funky, fermented soybean paste hails from Japan but is now widely available everywhere. Here it works wonders alongside the other flavor bombs, helping to build one supremely tasty sauce that always manages to elevate everything with which it comes into contact.

Makes about 1 cup

2 teaspoons olive oil
⅓ cup diced onion
2 large garlic cloves, minced
¼ cup apple cider vinegar
1 tablespoon molasses
2 tablespoons white miso
2 tablespoons maple syrup
1 cup plus 2 tablespoons ketchup

Heat the oil in a saucepan set over medium heat. When it is shimmering hot, add the onion and sauté until lightly golden. Add the garlic and cook for 30 seconds. Add the vinegar, molasses, miso, and maple syrup. Cook for 1 minute, stirring constantly. Add the ketchup and let the mixture simmer, covered, for 5 minutes.

Transfer everything to a blender and blend until totally smooth. Cool completely before transferring to a lidded storage container. This will keep in the refrigerator for up to 2 weeks.

Rainbow Brights

Part of the reason why I love these chard and carrot pickles so much is the fact that they're so stinkin' pretty. There, I admitted it. Shallow though my affections may be, I also adore these rainbow-colored jewels for their satisfying crunch and the mouth-puckering pop of acid that they lend to anything and everything. From salads and tacos to braises and soups, it's tough to find a plate or bowl that wouldn't be better for these prismatic pickles.

Makes 1 (32-ounce) jar

2 cups white distilled vinegar
2 cups filtered water
2 tablespoons kosher salt
2 tablespoons sugar
2 tablespoons mustard seeds
1 tablespoon coriander seeds
2 star anise

1 tablespoon whole black or pink peppercorns
2 bunches rainbow chard stems, cut into ¼-inch pieces
3 cups ¼-inch pieces rainbow carrots, peeled if you like

In a large pot over medium-high heat, combine the vinegar, water, salt, sugar, mustard seeds, coriander seeds, star anise, and peppercorns. Bring to a gentle boil and stir to blend. Once the sugar and salt have fully dissolved, turn off the heat and transfer the pickling liquid to a lidded 32-ounce jar. Add the chard stems and carrot pieces. Let this mixture cool to room temperature, cover with the lid, and store in the refrigerator for 4 to 6 weeks.

House Dressing

This is it. The one. My most trusted, well-worn, better-than-all-the-rest salad dressing that is truly great with just about everything. This recipe was inspired by a delicious dressing from Kat the Farmer in my hometown of Blacksburg, Virginia.

Makes about 1 cup

1 tablespoon white miso
2 tablespoons tahini
Juice of ½ large lemon
1 tablespoon apple
   cider vinegar
2 teaspoons maple syrup
¼ teaspoon garlic powder
¼ teaspoon nutritional yeast
Salt
Freshly ground black pepper
⅔ cup extra virgin olive oil

In a blender, combine the miso, tahini, lemon juice, vinegar, syrup, garlic powder, nutritional yeast, and salt and pepper to taste. Blend on high until very smooth. With the motor running, slowly drizzle in the oil until it has all been added. The dressing will be smooth and creamy (pourable, but just barely). Taste and adjust for seasoning. Transfer to a lidded jar or storage bottle and keep in the fridge for up to 3 weeks.

Salty Butter-Whipped Honey

Sounds sinful, right? I can assure you that this isn't nearly as rich as it sounds. This drippy, sticky-sweet thing is my lighter take on a simple honey butter where, instead of infusing a lot of butter with a little honey, we're going to infuse a lot of honey with a little butter. Just be sure to use a good-quality raw honey.

Makes about 1 cup

8 ounces honey
2 tablespoons salted butter,
   at room temperature
Salt to taste

In a blender, combine the honey, butter, and salt and blend until creamy and smooth. Transfer to a lidded storage jar or container. This buttery honey will keep in the refrigerator for up to 1 month.

Citrusy Poppy Seed Coleslaw

The term "slaw" is a very common, catchall sort of moniker, befitting any number of highly flavorful, veggie-packed gatherings. Beet slaw. Apple-jicama slaw. Brussels sprouts slaw . . . you can really "slaw" most anything if you put your mind to it. But here, I'm sharing a mostly classic take on a cabbage-based coleslaw, whose bright, tangy notes are tempered by some earthy, slightly gritty tahini and a showering of micro-crunching poppy seeds. It's not very sweet, this slaw, but I suppose you could go heavier on that part if you like.

P. S. My mom always puts cucumber in her coleslaw, and she knows best.

Makes 6 to 8 servings

½ English cucumber, diced (no need to peel or seed)
1 (16-ounce) bag coleslaw mix
1 (8-ounce) bag bean sprouts (optional)
2 scallions, white and green parts, finely chopped
1 cup plain Greek or regular yogurt
1 tablespoon honey or maple syrup
1 tablespoon tahini
1 tablespoon poppy seeds
Zest and juice of 1 lemon
Zest and juice of 1 lime
2 teaspoons apple cider vinegar
1 teaspoon garlic powder
Salt
Freshly ground black pepper

In a large mixing bowl, combine the diced cucumber, coleslaw mix, sprouts (if using), and scallions.

In a smaller mixing bowl, stir together the yogurt, honey, tahini, poppy seeds, lemon and lime zest and juice, vinegar, and garlic powder. Pour the mixture over the slaw ingredients and toss enthusiastically until everything is well coated. Taste and season with salt and pepper.

Cover and store in the refrigerator for up to 1 week.

FIRST LIGHTS

*Breakfast is to the Southern table as
a mirror ball is to a dance floor.*

*On the surface, just a simple collection
of everyday things, but it can be
fancy, too, depending on how you
look at it, where you stand.*

*What you ultimately choose is
a small reflection of you,
a piece of your whole routine.*

*It will get you moving, pulling you up and out
from under covers,
beckoning.*

*Making it a little bit easier to
get up and go.*

*To rise
and shine.*

Vanilla Cream-Stuffed Baked Beignets

Fluffy, cloudlike pillows of lightly sweetened dough—that's what you'll end up with here, with these easy and (dare I say) foolproof baked beignets. This lighter riff on the classic New Orleans sweet treat is more like a cross between a soft roll and a beignet. As such, I highly suggest stuffing them with a luscious whipped cream to really double down on the whole doughnut vibe.

A snowfall of powdered sugar is an absolute must, of course. They simply would not be beignets without it.

Makes about 30 beignets

¾ cup lukewarm water
½ cup plus 2 tablespoons maple syrup, at room temperature
1 heaping teaspoon active dry yeast
1 large egg, at room temperature, beaten
½ teaspoon salt
1 teaspoon ground cinnamon (optional)

2 teaspoons vanilla extract
½ cup buttermilk, at room temperature
2 tablespoons melted coconut oil or ghee, plus more for oiling
3½ cups white whole wheat flour
1 recipe Yogurty Whipped Cream (page 21)
Powdered sugar, for dusting

SPECIAL EQUIPMENT
piping tip

In a large mixing bowl, whisk together the water with the maple syrup and yeast. Let this sit for 10 minutes. In a separate bowl, whisk together the beaten egg, salt, cinnamon (if using), vanilla, and buttermilk.

Pour the egg mixture into the yeast mixture and whisk. Switch to a wooden spoon to add the coconut oil and flour, and stir until everything is well combined. Transfer the (very sticky) dough to a lightly oiled bowl, cover with plastic wrap, and let it rise for at least 2 hours or overnight.

Line 2 baking sheets with parchment paper.

Transfer the proofed dough onto a clean work surface and roll it into a roughly ¼-inch-thick rectangle. Cut the beignets into approximately 2-inch squares (a pizza cutter is great for this). Evenly divide the beignets between the prepared baking sheets, ensuring there is about 1 inch of space between each one.

Let the beignets rise for 1 hour, uncovered.

Meanwhile, preheat the oven to 350°F. Adjust the rack to the middle position. Make sure there is still some space between each beignet, and bake for 12 to 14 minutes, or until golden.

While the beignets are baking, spoon the whipped cream into a large zip-top bag or a decorating bag that is fitted with a piping tip. Snip the corner that is fitted with the piping tip just enough so you can pipe the cream.

When they are cool enough to handle, push the piping tip about halfway into one end of each beignet and gently squeeze, filling them as much or as little as you like—just take care not to overstuff as they could burst.

Shower the stuffed beignets with powdered sugar and enjoy.

Herby Potato and Salmon Hash

The recipes in this chapter are largely here to push the boundaries of our ordinary breakfast-ing. I wanted to give you some different food for thought, literally. Enter this salmon and potato recipe, which tips its hat to some of my favorite bagel fixin's but by any other name is basically a hash.

Makes 4 servings

SPOTLIGHT

Don't care for the white stuff that oozes out of cooked salmon? I get it. But it's just a flavorless protein and is perfectly safe to eat. If you want to minimize it, you can soak your salmon fillets in a quick brine prior to cooking. In a baking dish, create a brine of 1 tablespoon of salt per every 1 cup of water. Stir to fully dissolve the salt and place the salmon in the brine for 15 minutes. Rinse and pat dry before using.

1 teaspoon baking soda
Salt
4 pounds Yukon Gold potatoes cut into 1-inch pieces (no need to peel)
4 tablespoons olive oil, divided
1 teaspoon garlic powder
Freshly ground black pepper
2 cups roughly chopped red onion, plus extra sliced onion for topping
3 bell peppers, mixed colors, roughly chopped
4 salmon fillets (either skinless or skin-on is fine)
Store-bought everything bagel seasoning blend
2 cups mixed fresh herbs, roughly chopped (I use parsley, chives, cilantro, and/or dill)

Preheat the oven to 450°F. Adjust 1 rack to the top third of the oven and another on the lower third. Cover 2 large baking sheets with parchment paper.

Fill a large pot two thirds full with water. Sprinkle in the baking soda and generously salt the water. Bring to a boil and add the potatoes. Cook until fork-tender, about 25 minutes.

Drain and return the potatoes to the pot. Put the lid on and give them a good shake to bust them up a bit, releasing the mushy, creamy insides. Add 3 tablespoons of the oil to the potatoes, then the garlic powder, a teaspoon or so of salt, and lots of black pepper. Stir to coat.

Transfer the seasoned potatoes to the first prepared baking sheet. Roast on the top rack, stirring once halfway through, for 35 to 40 minutes, or until fantastically golden brown and crispy.

During the last 10 minutes of the potatoes' cooking time, add the chopped onions and bell peppers to half of the second pan, then season lightly with salt and pepper. Put the salmon fillets on the other side, and sprinkle with the bagel seasoning. Drizzle with the remaining 1 tablespoon of oil. Roast on the lower rack for 8 to 9 minutes, or until the salmon is just done and flakes easily with a fork.

Serve the salmon with the potatoes, onions, and peppers. Shower the herbs over top, and add sliced red onion.

Crunchy Cinnamon Toast

Save for the molasses, this recipe isn't particularly Southern—I'll cop to that. But it is particularly delicious, so covered in nostalgia that I can't not share it with you. Over the years, I've found ways to preserve the decadent soul of this toast while lightening it up significantly (there's no butter). This toast is just sneaky good and is easily multiplied.

Makes 4 slices

SPOTLIGHT

Unrefined coconut oil retains the natural coconutty flavor, and it is delicious if you're into that sort of thing. If not, you can substitute canola, grapeseed, or vegetable oil.

½ cup maple syrup
1 ½ teaspoons ground cinnamon, divided
2 teaspoons molasses
1 teaspoon vanilla extract or vanilla bean paste
2 tablespoons brown sugar

1 tablespoon turbinado sugar, plus more for sprinkling
Unrefined coconut oil, for spreading and cooking (see Spotlight; I typically use about ¼ cup)
4 slices whole-grain bread

In a small saucepan over medium heat, combine the maple syrup with ½ teaspoon of the cinnamon and the molasses. Bring to a gentle boil, stirring to mix, and then turn off the heat. Add the vanilla and stir well.

In a medium bowl or on a plate, combine the brown sugar, the remaining 1 teaspoon of cinnamon, and the turbinado sugar. Feel free to add more cinnamon if you like.

Spoon about 2 tablespoons of coconut oil into a large (preferably nonstick) skillet set over medium heat, and allow it to fully melt. Add the bread slices to the pan, working in batches as needed, and toast on both sides until light golden brown and, well, toasty.

Transfer the toast to a baking sheet and brush 1 side of each piece of bread liberally with the maple-cinnamon syrup, ensuring that you get the whole surface area nice and soaked. Sprinkle the soaked sides of each slice with the brown sugar–cinnamon mixture, creating a generous crust. Sprinkle each slice with a little turbinado sugar, if desired.

Add another tablespoon of coconut oil to the pan and, cinnamon-sugar sides facing down, toast the bread slices over medium heat just until the sugars caramelize and begin to brown nicely; 20 to 30 seconds (this goes fast). We're just toasting that sugared side this time, so once you've got it cooked to your liking, transfer the toast slices to a platter or to serving plates.

Repeat with any remaining slices, making sure to wipe down the skillet between batches to avoid burning the sugars. Enjoy warm.

Smoky Pinto Beans with Vinegared Tomatoes

When it comes to deliciously simple, unfussed with country cooking, there may be no better representative than Southern-style pinto beans. Costing pennies to make and consisting of only a few wholesome ingredients, a humble pot of ham hock–flavored pintos simmering away on the stove says "home" to so many Southerners. In this spin, which also resembles a full English breakfast, I'm using canned pinto beans, so we don't have to take the time to soak dried ones. We'll also forgo the ham hocks and crisp up some presliced country ham instead. Because it's so flavorful, I find that you only need one or two slices of ham per serving; a little goes a long way. In fact, I almost treat it more like a seasoning. You could also skip the ham altogether for a vegan version that is still a remarkably balanced plate of flavors and textures.

Makes 4 servings

1 cup balsamic vinegar
6 ounces country ham "biscuit slices" or prosciutto
2 teaspoons olive oil, plus extra for drizzling
1 cup sliced sweet onion
1 chipotle pepper, minced, plus 2 teaspoons of the adobo sauce
3 garlic cloves, minced or grated
2 (15-ounce) cans pinto beans, drained and rinsed
Salt
Freshly ground black pepper
2 large tomatoes, sliced

Pour the vinegar into a small saucepan over medium heat. Let it simmer until it has reduced by close to half; this takes about 15 minutes. It should thicken and get sticky, and it will continue to thicken as it cools. Set aside.

Meanwhile, place a deep skillet over medium heat. Working in batches as needed, place the ham slices into the pan to heat through and crisp up; this takes about 1 minute total, flipping once halfway through. Transfer the crisped slices to a plate. (Don't wipe out the pan! The ham seasoned it for you.)

Pour the oil into the same pan, still over medium heat. When it's hot, add the onion. Sauté until very tender, 5 to 7 minutes, stirring frequently. Add the chipotle, adobo sauce, and garlic and cook for 1 minute more, stirring occasionally. Add the beans and allow them to warm through, stirring to mix. Season everything to taste with a good amount of salt and pepper.

Arrange the sliced tomatoes on a plate or in a bowl. Drizzle with some of the reduced vinegar and season them with salt and pepper. Serve the beans over the vinegared tomatoes and nestle the crisped country ham all around. Finish with a drizzle of olive oil, if you like. (I like.)

Eggs Sardou, Sort Of

Created at Antoine's in New Orleans's French Quarter, this classic Cajun-Creole dish just has good bones. Traditionally speaking, poached eggs are served atop buttered artichoke hearts and creamed spinach, and it's all covered in a warm blanket of rich hollandaise sauce. In my lighter, healthy spin on the original, we'll make a big pan of lemony, slightly spicy spinach and artichoke hearts and a velvety tahini yogurt. Jammy soft-boiled egg yolks provide all the sauce you need for this nutritious flavor-packed breakfast that, admittedly, also resembles a spinach-artichoke dip—in the best way.

Makes 4 servings

4 large eggs
2 tablespoons olive oil
5 large garlic cloves, sliced into thin "chips" (not minced)
Chopped scallions, green and white parts separated
10 ounces fresh baby spinach
4 thin slices fresh lemon
Salt
Freshly ground black pepper
1 teaspoon red pepper flakes or ¼ teaspoon cayenne (optional)
6 ounces marinated artichoke hearts, drained and roughly chopped
1 cup plain Greek yogurt
1½ tablespoons tahini

Put a large pot of water over high heat and bring to a boil. When boiling, add the eggs (very carefully) and boil for exactly 6 minutes. Transfer them to a bowl of ice water. When they're cool enough to handle, carefully peel away the shells and cut them in half, exposing the soft, jammy yolks. Set aside.

In a large, deep nonstick skillet set over medium heat, combine the oil and garlic slices. Allow the garlic to gently toast in the oil, stirring and tossing occasionally until golden brown, 3 to 4 minutes. Transfer the garlic to a small bowl and set aside, leaving the flavored oil in the pan.

With the heat still on medium, add the scallion whites, spinach, lemon, salt and black pepper to taste, and the red pepper flakes to the garlicky oil and cook, stirring frequently, for 3 to 4 minutes, until the spinach is tender and wilted. Add the artichoke hearts and let them warm through.

In a small bowl, combine the yogurt and tahini, seasoning with salt and pepper to taste. Spread this mixture on a large plate or serving platter. Top with the lemony greens and artichoke hearts mixture and the soft-boiled eggs. Garnish with the chopped scallion greens and reserved garlic chips.

Peachy Pecan Pie Pancake

At some point along the road of my home cooking adventures, my search for the perfect pancakes dissolved into my happy discovery of the perfect pancake. A single slice is all you need to satisfy—no giant, tranquilizing stacks need apply. This was revelatory for me. The maple syrup will coax the natural sugars out of the peaches, creating a sticky-sweet topping. In this lightened-up, butter-free version, the protein-rich batter rises and puffs up beautifully in the oven, hugging the peaches almost as if to say, "It's going to be one very good morning."

Makes 4 servings

4 tablespoons vegetable oil, canola oil, or ghee, divided
4 large eggs
⅔ cup milk
⅔ cup white whole wheat flour
2 teaspoons vanilla bean paste or vanilla extract
½ teaspoon ground cinnamon
¼ teaspoon kosher salt
1 ripe peach, thinly sliced
1 cup pecan halves
2 tablespoons maple syrup, plus more for serving
Fresh raspberries (optional)

Preheat the oven to 450°F. Adjust the rack to the middle position. Pour 2 tablespoons of the oil in a 10-inch ovenproof skillet or baking dish. Place the skillet in the oven for 3 minutes.

In a blender, combine the eggs, milk, flour, vanilla, cinnamon, salt, and the remaining 2 tablespoons of oil. Blend on high speed until the batter is very smooth, making sure there are no large clumps of flour left.

Carefully remove the hot skillet from the oven and pour in the batter. Bake for 20 to 25 minutes, or until the pancake is fully puffed and browned on top. Be sure not to open the oven during baking, or you'll risk deflating the pancake.

Meanwhile, in a large skillet over medium heat, combine the peach slices and pecans. Drizzle with the maple syrup and stir to coat. Cook the peaches and pecans until tender, lightly browned, and sticky (you shouldn't need oil for this, but if things stick too much, a little bit is fine).

Remove the pancake from the oven and top with the sticky peaches and pecans. Serve with extra maple syrup and raspberries, if desired.

Spiced Pork Tenderloin with Apples and Onion

From bacon and country ham to old-fashioned breakfast sausage, pork has long enjoyed a prominent spot on Southern breakfast and brunch tables. This recipe makes itself right at home in that tradition, but in a lighter, less greasy way. Here, we're giving a nod to both breakfast sausage and Southern grillades, which are medallions of either steak or pork that have been slowly simmered in gravy until fork-tender. To speed things up a bit, and to keep this recipe comfortably on the lighter side, we're going to roll a lean pork tenderloin in some traditional sausage seasonings, giving it a flavorful spiced crust, and then we'll roast it alongside some apples and sweet onion. This makes for one intensely satisfying plate that I especially love to serve for brunch.

Makes 4 servings

Natural nonstick cooking spray (I use coconut oil spray)
3 apples, thickly sliced (any variety you like to cook with or have on hand)
1 sweet onion, sliced into petals
Olive oil
Salt
Freshly ground black pepper
1 tablespoon whole fennel seeds, finely chopped or ground
3 teaspoons poultry seasoning
½ teaspoon garlic powder
½ cup Dijon mustard
1½ tablespoons maple syrup
1¼- to 1½-pound pork tenderloin
½ to ⅔ cup frizzled sage leaves (see Note) (optional)

Preheat the oven to 425°F. Adjust the rack to the middle position. Spray a 9 x 13-inch baking dish with cooking spray.

Spread out the sliced apples and onion in the baking dish. Drizzle with a little oil to coat and season with salt and pepper to taste. Toss to mix.

In a small bowl, combine the fennel seeds, poultry seasoning, garlic powder, and salt and pepper to taste. In a second small bowl, stir together the mustard and maple syrup. Brush about 1 tablespoon of the mustard mixture all over the pork and then coat evenly with the fennel mixture. Lay the pork over the apples and onion in the dish.

Roast for 25 minutes, or until the pork has reached an internal temperature of 145°F. Remove the dish from the oven, cover with foil, and let the pork rest and carryover cook for 10 minutes before slicing into thin medallions.

Serve the sliced pork with the apples and onion, and the remaining mustard mixture as a dipping sauce. Top with frizzled sage leaves , if using.

Note To frizzle sage leaves (I love that verb), just put a thin layer of cooking oil in a small skillet, and when it's shimmering hot, cook the fresh sage leaves for 20 to 30 seconds per side, or just until they're visibly beginning to brown. Transfer to a paper towel–lined plate to drain. They'll become shatteringly crispy as they cool.

Crunchy Coconut-Pineapple "Doughnuts"

Don't let the name fool you—there's no actual dough involved in this recipe, nor is there any frying for that matter. This is merely a different way to wield two of my favorite, can't-get-enough-of-them flavors: coconut and pineapple. We'll coat fresh pineapple slices with a glaze of sticky-sweet honey and some unsweetened coconut flakes, along with a bit of lime. A quick trip through the oven will yield a lightly browned, crunchy crust and just-tender fruit. When autumn rolls around, this also works beautifully with Delicata squash.

Makes about 8 "doughnuts"

2 cups unsweetened coconut flakes

½ cup superfine almond flour

1 scant teaspoon ground cinnamon

Zest of 1 lime

1 pineapple, peeled, cored, and cut into ¼- to ½-inch-thick rings

Honey, for brushing

Natural nonstick cooking spray

Edible flowers (optional)

Preheat the oven to 350°F. Adjust the rack to the middle position. Put a piece of parchment paper or a silicone baking mat on a large baking sheet.

Pulse the coconut flakes in a food processor to break up into more of a coconut dust. Pour this into a bowl, and add the almond flour, cinnamon, and lime zest.

Brush each pineapple ring with a thin layer of honey and then coat thickly with the coconut mixture, pressing it into the surface so it sticks. Put each coated pineapple ring onto the prepared baking sheet. Carefully spray the "doughnuts" evenly with some cooking spray (this will help with browning and crunch).

Bake for 12 minutes, just until the coconut looks evenly golden brown all over and the pineapple is warmed and tender. Let the pineapple rest for at least 5 minutes before enjoying. If you like, sprinkle a few edible flowers on top before serving.

Any Beans and Greens Breakfast Soup

Only recently have I begun to consider the idea of adding warming, nourishing bone broth (it's just stock, y'all) to my standard breakfast bowls. This simple move transforms a ragtag bowl of greens and things into an utterly satisfying meal. Breakfast soups are widely enjoyed in other corners of the world, but they are not so common on breakfast tables in the American South. With this one, I've taken some inspiration from the region's vast range of vegetable soups and stews, settling on a recipe that is enticing enough to lure me out of bed and hearty enough to keep me going for hours. Plus, adding a Parmesan rind to soups is a great way to coax out a ton of cheesy, savory flavor without actually adding any cheese. You can make a double batch of this soup, and then enjoy a hot, energizing breakfast all week long.

Makes 4 servings

2 tablespoons olive oil
1½ cups diced sweet onion
1 tablespoon chicken or beef stock concentrate
20 ounces fresh greens, roughly chopped (such as kale, collards, turnip, chard, and/or spinach)
1 garlic clove, smashed
2 (15-ounce) cans beans (pinto, great northern, butter, etc.), drained
2 tablespoons balsamic or apple cider vinegar
Salt
Freshly ground black pepper
32 ounces low-sodium chicken or beef bone broth
1 Parmesan cheese rind
Poached or soft-boiled eggs, for serving
Rainbow Brights (page 26), for serving

Pour the oil into a large Dutch oven set over medium heat. Add the onion and stock concentrate and sauté until tender, about 5 minutes. Add the greens and garlic and cook, stirring frequently, until wilted and very tender, 4 to 8 minutes, depending on which green you chose (the heartier greens take longer to cook).

Add the beans and vinegar and stir to combine. Season with salt and pepper to taste.

Add the bone broth and the Parmesan rind, cover, reduce the heat to low, and allow the soup to simmer for 10 minutes. The longer it simmers, the more tender the greens will be and the flavor of the broth will continue to deepen. Serve with eggs and/or rainbow brights.

SPOTLIGHT

Freeze individual servings of soup in reusable freezer bags, and thaw and reheat in pots of simmering water until warmed through. This is also delicious served over grits or Savory Cheddar Waffled Oatmeal (page 51).

Porridge Three Ways

If the word "porridge" doesn't make you want to drop everything you're doing and sprint to the table, spoon in hand, I get it. It is among the more unfortunate monikers in the food world, eliciting groans, furrowed brows, and quizzical expressions from my crew when I announce that it's what's on the docket for breakfast. But a porridge can be so many things, as it's really more of a category of food than any specific recipe. Oatmeal, by any other name, is a porridge. Same goes for grits and cream of wheat (something I ate by the bucketload as a kid). This genre of food, what with all of its wholesome grains, warming comforts, and endless flavor possibilities, makes an ideal canvas for breakfast riffing. The next three recipes—one savory and two sweet—are here to showcase the possibilities of porridge and to inspire you to fill your breakfast tables with hearty, warm bowls of it. Defined as "providing abundant nourishment," hearty food is by no means synonymous with heavy food. These recipes are filled with whole, good-for-you ingredients that will work for you, not against you, leaving you feeling satisfied and full for hours.

Maple-Molasses Grits with Salty, Slumped Fruit

When I find myself seeking a sweeter bite in the morning, I tend to steer my craving down roads that lead to things just like this—creamy, naturally sweetened grits piled high with roasted, maple-caramelized fruit. For me, South Carolina peaches are usually the ticket, but almost any fruit will do, from apples and pears to berries of all shapes and sizes. Just adjust the roast time as needed. The ingredient list here is small yet mighty, a collection of simple, plant-based, whole foods that work so well together they'll have you thinking you're doing something naughty.

Makes 6 to 8 servings

2 cups sliced ripe fruit (stone fruit, pears, and apples are my favorite)
3 tablespoons plus ½ cup maple syrup, divided
Salt
1 cup water
2 cups milk
1½ cups quick-cooking grits (white or yellow)
2 teaspoons molasses
2 teaspoons vanilla extract or vanilla bean paste
1 teaspoon ground cinnamon

In a large nonstick skillet over medium heat, combine the fruit and 3 tablespoons of the maple syrup. Season with salt to taste and cook until the fruit is just tender and slumped, 2 to 3 minutes.

Meanwhile, pour the water and milk into a medium saucepan and bring to a boil. Add the grits in a slow-steady stream, whisking while you do. Reduce the heat to medium-low and cook until the grits are thick and creamy, stirring frequently.

Turn off the heat and add the remaining ½ cup of maple syrup, the molasses, vanilla, and cinnamon. Stir to combine.

Spoon some of the grits into a bowl, or onto a large platter for family style, and pile some of the sticky fruit on top.

Note *For extra richness and creaminess, stir in 1 or 2 tablespoons of coconut butter.*

continued»

Peanut Butter–Oatmeal Breakfast Cookies

I ate a sizable bowl of strawberry ice cream for breakfast once. As an adult. I'm not sure what inspired that choice, but it was clearly inspired. Mostly, I think my craving for something sweet was so fierce that I skipped right over all of the sensible options (there are so many sensible options) and went straight to the mother lode. Happy as it made me in that moment, I didn't feel great the rest of that morning. Imagine that. This recipe is also inspired, but more responsibly so, and I can't tell you how happy your morning can be when you kick it off with something playful like these healthy, reduced-sugar cookies. They live in the same land as wholesome cereals and breakfast bars. But here, we'll see those bars and raise them up and into full-on cookie territory. Because a breakfast cookie trumps a breakfast bar.

Makes 10 to 12 cookies

1½ cups old-fashioned rolled oats
⅓ cup whole wheat flour
1 teaspoon baking soda
1 teaspoon ground cinnamon
⅔ cup natural peanut butter
¼ cup coconut oil, melted
¼ cup maple syrup
⅔ cup brown sugar or coconut sugar
2 tablespoons molasses
1 large egg

Preheat the oven to 350°F. Line 2 baking sheets with parchment paper or silicone baking mats.

In a large bowl, mix together the oats, flour, baking soda, and cinnamon. Stir well to thoroughly combine.

In a food processor, combine the peanut butter, coconut oil, maple syrup, brown sugar, molasses, and egg. Process for several seconds to blend well, and then add this mixture to the oat mixture. Stir well to evenly distribute. The dough will be very thick.

Roll heaping tablespoons of the dough into balls and evenly space them on the prepared baking sheets, keeping them about 2 inches apart. Bake for 8 to 9 minutes, or until golden brown and set.

Cool completely before storing. These will keep covered in a cool, dry place for up to 5 days.

Savory Cheddar Waffled Oatmeal

This recipe stretches the boundaries of what a bowl of oatmeal can be. In fact, we're ditching the bowl altogether. I tinkered around with my go-to savory oatmeal recipe one day (as one does), the results of which have bettered—and battered—my mornings ever since. I found that oatmeal is actually the perfect thing to waffle (this is also a verb today), and it's even more delicious when you add just a little bit of extra-sharp cheddar cheese, some pickled jalapeños, and if you desire, a sunny-side-up egg.

Makes about 4 (4-inch) waffles

4 cups vegetable or
  chicken stock
2 cups quick-cooking oats
2 teaspoons salt
Freshly ground black pepper
¾ cup extra-sharp cheddar
  cheese (the sharper
  the flavor, the less
  you need to use)
¼ cup whole wheat flour

Chopped scallions, white and
  green parts, separated
2 large eggs, beaten
Natural nonstick cooking spray
10 to 12 pickled jalapeños
Fried eggs, for serving
Sliced avocados, for serving
Scorned-Women Hot Sauce
  (page 24), for serving

SPECIAL EQUIPMENT
  a waffle iron

Pour the stock into a medium saucepan and bring it to a boil. Add the oats, salt, and pepper to taste and cook, stirring, until smooth and creamy, about 5 minutes. Turn off the heat and stir in the cheese, flour, scallion whites, and the eggs.

Preheat a waffle iron and spray with cooking spray.

Spoon half of the oatmeal batter into the waffle iron and top with some of the pickled jalapeños. Cook according to the manufacturer's directions, until the steaming has stopped; 4 to 5 minutes total. Transfer the cooked waffle to a plate or serving platter and repeat with the remaining batter.

Serve the waffles with fried eggs, chopped scallion greens, sliced avocados, and a little hot sauce.

SEA LIGHTS

She sells sea shells.

They'll cost you about two sand dollars apiece.

Sea spray tickles her nose, sends her hair flying.

"I'm still hungry," she says, licking salty
fingers. "Seafood tastes better by the water."

"Is that so?"
"Yes. It's not homesick yet. Seasick?"

Skipping through foamy waters, she belts,
"I'm the Queen of Carolina! Her Royal
Highness of the Low Country Coastline."

The Princess of Tides.

Her eyes like glassy portholes scan the story-
haunted waters, hoping for mermaids,

for sea monsters
for Blackbeard's ship.

Daylight fades as she keeps watch,
safe behind her castle of sand.

The rising tides wash away any evidence
of our oceanside picnic, erasing all tracks,
with their endless ebb and flow.

Gilded by the sun.
Guided by the moon.

Pan-Seared Oysters in a Buttermilk Remoulade Bath

I have to believe that moving to the Low Country would make an oyster lover out of just about anyone. It's certainly proven true for me. Even just the occasions that tend to revolve around oysters and their preparation are enough to charm even the most dedicated haters. Whether raw and thrown back with a bucket of ice-cold beers or fried crispy and piled on top of a fresh roll, I'll take them any which way they're shucked and shared.

Here, oysters are cooked up quickly with a flavorful remoulade-inspired sauce (no mayo here, though). But the most important thing is to get the freshest oysters you can find. If you can't get your hands on any, just substitute shrimp or scallops. It will be delicious all the same.

Makes 4 servings as a starter or 2 as a main

4 teaspoons olive oil, divided
10 to 12 fresh raw oysters, shucked
Salt
Freshly ground black pepper
1 shallot, minced
1 tablespoon capers
2 garlic cloves, minced or grated
1 tablespoon Creole mustard
2 tablespoons chili sauce or ketchup
1 to 2 teaspoons prepared horseradish
1 tablespoon Worcestershire sauce
¾ cup buttermilk
Watercress, for garnish (optional)
Toasted bread, oyster crackers, or saltines, for serving

Pour 2 teaspoons of the oil into a large skillet set over medium heat. When it's hot, add the oysters to the pan. Season with salt and pepper to taste and cook for 3 to 4 minutes on the first side, and then 2 to 3 minutes on the second side. Transfer to a plate and set aside.

Pour the remaining 2 teaspoons of oil into the pan, still over medium heat. Add the shallot and capers and cook, stirring occasionally, for about 2 minutes. Add the garlic and cook for 30 seconds more.

Add the mustard, chili sauce, horseradish, Worcestershire sauce, and buttermilk. Season with salt and pepper to taste. Stir and let the sauce thicken and reduce for 2 to 3 minutes. Put the oysters back in the pan and let them simmer in the sauce for 1 to 2 minutes, just until they're fully cooked (when their edges begin to curl, they've overcooked, so try to avoid that and you should be good to go).

Garnish with watercress, if using, and serve right away with bread or crackers.

Viet-Cajun Seafood Broil
with Chili-Garlic Oil

Not to go playing favorites, but when it comes to the recipes in this book—this one might be it. The one. This favoritism is linked to the simple fact that this recipe has everything I want when I sit down to a meal: perfectly cooked shrimp and savory sausage, bursts of slightly charred sweet corn, salty potatoes (a way of life all on their own), and the most flavor-packed garlicky, spicy sauce with which to drench the aforementioned crew. There's not much more to say about it—I could happily eat this every day. Inspired by the culturally rich and utterly delicious food scene in my brother's home city of Houston, this recipe also tips its hat to the Low Country seafood boils that frequent the coastline I call home.

Makes 4 servings

FOR THE SEAFOOD BROIL

24-ounces baby yellow potatoes, halved
Olive oil, for cooking
Kosher salt
Freshly ground black pepper
4 smoked chicken sausage links
4 fresh ears of corn
1 to 1½ pounds fresh shrimp, peeled and deveined
Chopped fresh cilantro, watercress, and/or scallions (optional)
Freshly cut limes, for serving

FOR THE CHILI-GARLIC OIL

2 teaspoons lemongrass paste (from your grocer's fresh herbs section)
1-inch knob fresh ginger, peeled and grated or minced
3 large garlic cloves, minced or grated
2 teaspoons honey
1 tablespoon soy sauce
1½ teaspoons fish sauce
2 teaspoons chili-garlic sauce or sriracha
⅔ cup olive oil, or to taste

To make the seafood broil: Preheat the oven to 400°F. Adjust the racks to the top and middle positions. Cover 2 large baking sheets with parchment paper.

Put the potatoes on the first prepared baking sheet. Toss with enough oil to fully coat and season with salt and pepper to taste. Roast for 10 minutes on the middle rack, stir the potatoes, and add the sausages to the pan. Roast for about 20 minutes more, or until the potatoes are golden brown and crispy and the sausages are nice and browned.

Put the corn on the second prepared baking sheet and coat with oil and a little salt and pepper. Roast for 20 minutes on the top rack.

Toss the shrimp with enough oil to coat, and season with salt and pepper to taste.

After the corn has roasted for 20 minutes, put the shrimp on the same pan as the corn in an even layer. Broil for 4 to 5

minutes on the top rack, or until the shrimp are just done (it's fine if the potatoes/sausages are still cooking at this point).

To make the chili-garlic oil: In a medium bowl, combine the lemongrass paste, ginger, garlic, honey, soy sauce, fish sauce, chili-garlic sauce, and oil until well mixed. Taste and adjust as you like.

Transfer the cooked sausages, shrimp, and vegetables to a large platter or pile everything up on the same baking sheet (usually what I do). Toss with a generous amount of the chili-garlic oil, and top with chopped cilantro, watercress, and scallions (if using), and cut lime wedges. Serve with extra chili oil on the side for dunking and drizzling.

Crispy Scallops with Tomatoey Mignonette Vinaigrette

A classic oyster topping makes itself right at home in a pan of simply seared scallops. The addition of sun-dried tomatoes to the mix might be a very nineties thing to do, but I love the way they soften as they warm up, sweetening and standing up to the punchy vinegar-laced pan sauce.

Piling seared scallops on top a bed of baby spinach is fairly unoriginal, but I like to add a ton of whole, fresh basil leaves to the mix—a ratio of two parts spinach to one part basil. Pushing basil into the spotlight like this is a little surprising, and it steers an otherwise vintage recipe in a fresh, new direction.

Makes 4 servings

16 ounces sea scallops (12 to 14 scallops)
Salt
Freshly ground black pepper
¼ cup plus 1 tablespoon olive oil, divided
2 shallots, minced
¾ cup chopped sun-dried tomatoes
2 garlic cloves, minced or grated
2 to 3 tablespoons sherry vinegar or champagne vinegar, or to taste
4 cups baby spinach
2 cups chopped fresh basil

Pat the scallops dry with a paper towel and season all over with salt and pepper to taste.

Pour about 1 tablespoon of the oil in a large skillet set over medium-high heat. When it's hot, add the scallops in a single layer, working in batches if necessary. Let the scallops cook undisturbed until they're brown and crispy on 1 side, 4 to 5 minutes. Transfer the scallops to a plate for now (we'll finish cooking them in a sec). Drain and wipe out the skillet, and return it to the stovetop.

Working over medium heat now, add the remaining ¼ cup of oil to the pan. Add the shallots and tomatoes. Sauté for 3 to 4 minutes, until tender. Season lightly with salt and pepper.

Add the garlic and vinegar and cook for about 1 minute, just until warmed through. Return the scallops to the pan, browned sides facing up, and let them finish cooking in the vinegary sauce; this will take another 1 minute or so.

Meanwhile, put the spinach and basil on a big platter or divide them among individual plates. Toss them to mix. Top with the warm scallops and vinaigrette.

Hush Puppy Popovers

There are few Southern seafood-centric situations in which baskets or bowls of freshly fried hush puppies aren't present. Slathered in honey butter and enjoyed one after the other, hush puppies are essentially savory cornbread doughnuts served alongside your meal. Tasty, but not very healthy. For a lighter change of pace, I've got an easy cornmeal popover option here for you. The cornmeal gives my classic blender popover recipe a golden hue and a sturdier bite, and it's hard not to love the fact that these bake up in muffin tins—no popover pans need apply.

Makes 12 popovers

3 tablespoons ghee, olive oil, or liquid coconut oil, divided

3 large eggs

1 ½ cups buttermilk

1 ½ teaspoons salt

¾ cup plain yellow cornmeal

½ cup white whole wheat or all-purpose flour

Watercress, for garnish (optional)

Salty Butter–Whipped Honey (page 28), for serving

Preheat the oven to 450°F. Adjust the rack to the middle position.

Brush each of 12 muffin cups with some of the ghee, using up about 2 tablespoons' worth. When the oven is preheated, put the prepared muffin pan inside and let it heat up for 5 minutes.

In a blender, combine the remaining 1 tablespoon of ghee and the eggs, buttermilk, and salt.

In a small bowl, whisk together the cornmeal and the flour. Add this to the blender and blend until completely smooth. Remove the muffin pan from the oven and pour the batter into the greased muffin cups, filling them just over three-fourths full. Bake the popovers for 25 to 27 minutes, or until very golden brown and done in the centers. Garnish with watercress, if using, and serve with whipped honey.

Roasted Shrimp with Sweet Peas, Zucchini, and Oil-Toasted Pistachios

If you asked me to compose my perfect plate of food, it would look a whole lot like this. We're talking plump, exquisitely cooked shrimp (roasting is always the way), bursts of sweet green peas, crunchy raw zucchini, and a warm, garlicky toasted pistachio oil that is drinkably delicious. I could live in this recipe, to be honest, as it essentially ticks all of my major boxes: creamy, crunchy, warm, raw, salty, lemony, healthy. The yogurt is sort of optional, but dragging a warm salty shrimp through it is a highlight for me. I'll stop waxing on about it all, though, so you can join me here in my happy place.

Makes 4 servings

1 cup plain Greek yogurt
Zest of 1 lemon and the juice of half of it
Salt
Freshly ground black pepper
½ cup plus 1 tablespoon olive oil, divided
4 garlic cloves, smashed
½ cup chopped pistachios
½ teaspoon paprika
1½ pounds large shrimp, peeled and deveined
1 cup very thinly sliced zucchini (I use a mandoline)
1 (10-ounce) package steam-in-bag sweet peas, cooked according to package directions
Finely chopped chives, for garnish (optional)

Preheat the oven to 435°F. Adjust the oven rack to the middle position. Cover 1 baking sheet with parchment paper.

Combine the yogurt and lemon zest and juice in a small bowl and stir to combine. Season lightly with salt and pepper. Spread all over the bottom of a platter or divide it evenly among 4 plates.

Pour ½ cup of the oil into a saucepan set over medium heat. Add the smashed garlic, pistachios, and paprika. Let everything come to a light simmer and then reduce the heat to low. Cook gently for 5 minutes, until everything is toasty and golden. Remove from the heat and season with salt and pepper.

Put the shrimp on the prepared baking sheet, drizzle with the remaining 1 tablespoon of oil, and season with salt and pepper. Roast until just cooked, about 7 minutes. Toss the shrimp with the lemon zest.

To serve, pile the roasted shrimp on top of the lemony yogurt and tuck pieces of raw zucchini in and all around, followed by a sprinkling of sweet peas. Pour the warm pistachios and the oil (garlic included) all over everything, then sprinkle with the chopped chives, if using.

Seafood Stew with Toasted Garlic Broth

Here we have what is probably the most luxe recipe in this book, what with its bountiful collection of seafood, flavorful garlic broth, and creamy yogurt drizzle. Perfect for entertaining or for a chilly evening meal, this recipe is very easy to make and all comes together in one big covered pot, which, by definition, is what makes this stew a stew. The addition of chicken stock concentrate is reflective of many recipes I have on my website that seek to minimize time and effort. It is simply a fast and effective way to add big flavor to sauces, soups, and stews. A busy home cook's triumph, always.

Makes 4 to 6 servings

Olive oil, for cooking garlic
6 large garlic cloves, smashed
1 pound small red
   potatoes, quartered
Salt
Freshly ground black pepper
2 celery stalks, chopped,
   leaves reserved
1 large onion, diced
1 green bell pepper, diced
2 teaspoons Creole seasoning
1 tablespoon chicken
   stock concentrate or
   1 bouillon cube
½ cup white wine or sherry
6 cups chicken or seafood stock
1½ pounds fresh white
   fish fillets, such as
   snapper, grouper,
   tilapia, cod, or catfish
1 pound medium raw shrimp,
   peeled and deveined
1 cup plain Greek yogurt
Chopped fresh Italian
   parsley, chives and/or
   fresh dill, for garnishing

Pour in just enough oil to cover the bottom of a large Dutch oven set over medium heat. Add the garlic and let it gently simmer and tenderize in the hot oil. When it is fork-tender (squishy), it's done; this takes about 12 minutes, stirring frequently (it's worth it). Transfer the toasted garlic to a plate and set aside. Drain all but 2 tablespoons of the garlicky oil, and reserve for later (we'll use it!).

Add the potatoes to the pot with the oil, season with salt and pepper to taste, and cook for about 10 minutes (they get a head start). Add the celery, onion, bell pepper, and Creole seasoning. Sauté for 6 to 8 minutes, stirring occasionally, until everything is nice and tender.

Add the stock concentrate and wine and cook for about 1 minute. Mash up the toasted garlic with a fork until a paste forms, then add it to the pot. Add the stock and bring to a gentle simmer.

Add the fish and simmer, covered, for 3 minutes. Add the shrimp and simmer, covered, for 2 minutes more, or until just pink and curled (it goes really fast). Divide the fish and shrimp among serving bowls and ladle the broth and veggies over top.

Put the yogurt in a small bowl, season with salt and pepper to taste, and add a generous amount of the reserved garlic oil, until it is drizzle-able. Drizzle this garlicky, creamy mixture over the stew, and serve garnished with parsley, chives, and/or dill.

Sandbar Steamer

I'll see your platter of battered, greasy, deep-fried seafood and fries and raise you this much healthier spread. Inspired by a menu offering from a former favorite beachy haunt of mine (now closed), this recipe features my hack for steaming seafood and vegetables with just a pot and a colander—no bamboo steamer necessary. I don't own one, so I came up with this simple method as an alternative, and it works like a charm. The trick is transferring each steamed ingredient to a holding platter in a 170°F oven as the rest cook, so everything is nice and hot upon serving. Broccoli, potatoes, sausage, and fresh seafood go into the pot in an orderly procession, the salty water creating a steam that seasons the food as it cooks.

Makes 4 servings

12 to 16 ounces baby gold potatoes or small red potatoes
Sea salt
1 broccoli crown, cut into small florets
4 sausage links, cut into bite-size pieces, any kind you like (I go for kielbasa or andouille)
2 to 4 boneless, skinless fish fillets, such as triggerfish, salmon, cod, halibut, flounder, or grouper
Old Bay Seasoning
1 pound fresh clams, very well rinsed and drained of grit
Scorned-Women Hot Sauce (page 24) or Herby, Lemony Yogurt (page 21), for serving

Preheat the oven to warm (170°F). Adjust the rack to the middle position.

Put the potatoes into a large Dutch oven and add water to cover by 2 inches. Salt the water generously, like the sea. Put the pot over high heat and boil the potatoes for 10 minutes.

Put the broccoli florets and sausage into a colander or steamer basket and place down into the pot, right over the potatoes. Put the lid on the pot, making sure the colander is fully covered.

Steam the broccoli and sausage for 10 to 12 minutes, or until the veggies are tender. Remove the broccoli and sausage to a big platter (let the potatoes continue cooking) and keep it in the oven to stay warm while you prepare the seafood.

Put the clams in the colander. If you need to add more water, go for it. Put the lid on and steam the clams until they've fully opened, discarding any that don't, 6 to 8 minutes. Transfer to the platter with the veggies and keep in the warm oven.

Lastly, put the fish in the colander. Season with Old Bay to taste. Put the lid back on and steam for 5 minutes, or until the fish is opaque and flaky. Transfer the fish to the warm platter along with the potatoes, which should be very tender and fully cooked by now.

Serve with hot sauce, lemony yogurt, or any fixin's you like, and enjoy.

SPOTLIGHT

To make a great, fast crunchy chili oil, combine 3 teaspoons of chili-garlic paste with ¼ cup of olive oil (or any oil you like). Add ½ teaspoon of salt and a pinch of both sugar and toasted sesame seeds and/or black sesame seeds. Stir to combine, and adjust to your liking.

Tuna Salad with Roasted Lemon, Crunchy Potatoes, and Green Beans

Let's give heavy, mayonnaise-packed tuna salads a new spin—what do you say? Inspired by the Provençal-style Niçoise salad, this version features lightly seasoned canned tuna, the most incredible roasted potatoes, buttery lettuce, and tender-crisp green beans. Feel free to build upon these elements, if you like. Hard-boiled or poached eggs would be great, or some fresh green herbs, perhaps a few sweet, tiny tomatoes. But the real lesson in lighter cooking to be gleaned from this salad recipe is in the dressing of it all. The roasted lemon and a drizzle of healthy, fruity olive oil are all you need to make it sing. This is honestly true for almost everything you could classify as salad.

Makes 4 servings

1 teaspoon baking soda
Salt
6 cups (1-inch diced) gold potatoes
¼ cup plus 2 teaspoons olive oil, plus extra for dressing
Freshly ground black pepper
1 head butter lettuce, washed and trimmed
1 bunch fresh green beans, trimmed
2 lemons, sliced
2 cans solid albacore tuna, preferably packed in oil (this is the right time to use the good stuff)
1 shallot, thinly sliced

Preheat the oven to 425°F. Cover 2 large baking sheets with parchment paper.

Fill a large pot two-thirds full with water and add the baking soda. Salt the water generously (like ocean water) and bring to a boil. Add the potatoes and cook until completely fork-tender. Drain and return to the pot. Put the lid on and shake the potatoes to bust them up a bit, releasing their creamy insides. Add ¼ cup of the oil, a few teaspoons of salt, and lots of pepper. Toss gently to coat.

Spread the potatoes out on a prepared baking sheet in an even layer. Roast for 45 to 50 minutes, or until super crispy and very golden brown.

During the last 15 minutes of cooking, toss the green beans in the remaining 2 teaspoons of oil, season with salt and pepper to taste, add them to the second prepared baking sheet along with the lemon slices, and place in the oven.

Meanwhile, arrange the lettuce on a big platter or divide among 4 plates. Top with the tuna, followed by some of the roasted potatoes, green beans, and roasted lemons. Scatter some sliced shallots over top and finish with a drizzle of oil.

SPOTLIGHT

To eliminate some of the punchiness of the shallots, submerge the slices in a bowl of ice water for 5 minutes before using.

Southern Pickled Shrimp

Inspired by a now-retired menu item at a favorite Charleston restaurant, Edmund's Oast, this shrimp is a great back-pocket sort of recipe. Similar in some ways to Peruvian ceviche, this style of vinegary, marinated shrimp is classic in the South, and it's incredibly easy to make.

I take help from my local seafood shop (hi, Crosby's!) and purchase precooked fresh shrimp. The seafood counter in your go-to supermarket will have it, too. Feel free to riff on the ingredients here, adding and subtracting bits to make it yours. I love to pile the pickled shrimp and veggies on top of grilled and buttered wheat or rye toasts or I'll toss it with tons of simply cooked spaghetti squash for a light-yet-satisfying shrimp and "pasta salad" of sorts.

Makes 4 to 6 servings

⅔ cup thinly sliced red onion
1 large carrot or 8 to 10 baby carrots, thinly sliced
1 celery stalk, thinly sliced
1 to 1½ pounds cooked shrimp, peeled, deveined, and halved lengthwise
¼ cup capers
1 teaspoon celery seed
¾ cup champagne vinegar or apple cider vinegar
½ cup olive oil
1 teaspoon salt
Freshly ground black pepper
Tabasco or other hot sauce

In a large mixing bowl, combine the onion, carrots, celery, shrimp, capers, and celery seed.

In a small bowl or jar, whisk together the vinegar, oil, salt, pepper, and hot sauce. Pour this mixture into the bowl with the shrimp and vegetables and stir to coat. Cover and refrigerate for at least 2 hours before serving, stirring every so often. Let the shrimp sit outside of the fridge for at least 20 minutes before serving.

Mussels and Turnip Greens in Pickled Pepper Broth

Really, this recipe is just another way for me to enjoy two of my favorite things: mussels and greens. The addition of banana peppers to the mix serves a few different purposes here. Firstly, they add a nice color and crunch, as well as a nutritional boost to the dish. But most notably, they provide the very necessary burst of acidity that is so crucial to rounding out and balancing the inherent bitterness in dark leafy greens. I also like a pop of vinegary tang with my shellfish (classic), so it all just works. This is very hearty and doesn't necessarily require bread for sopping, but some crusty whole-grain crostini would be a beautiful thing to add. Just saying.

Makes 2 to 4 servings

1 tablespoon olive oil
1 shallot, minced
1 heaping cup pickled banana pepper rings, roughly chopped, plus 1 tablespoon pickling juice from the jar
3 large garlic cloves, minced or grated
½ cup dry white wine or sherry
10 ounces frozen turnip greens, thawed and squeezed of excess water
Salt
Freshly ground black pepper
2 ½ cups chicken stock, plus more as needed
1 pound fresh mussels, cleaned
Crusty whole-grain bread, for serving (optional)

Pour the oil into a large, deep skillet set over medium heat. When it's hot, add the shallot and banana peppers and cook, stirring, until the shallot is tender, 2 to 3 minutes. Add the garlic and cook for 30 seconds more.

Deglaze with the wine by adding it to the pan and letting it cook off for about 1 minute, stirring.

Add the greens and season with salt and pepper to taste. Add the stock, followed by the mussels. Bring to a bubble, cover, and simmer until the mussels have opened, 4 to 5 minutes. Discard any mussels that don't open and drizzle the banana pepper pickling liquid over the pan. Serve warm with crusty bread, for sopping, if desired.

SPOTLIGHT

While I love working with fresh ingredients, the convenience and efficiency of frozen greens can be a lifesaver sometimes. Frozen turnip greens and/or spinach work beautifully in this application, as the amount of fresh greens you'd have to purchase and cook down to equal what you get in a frozen package is . . . a lot.

DAY LIGHTS

When did I fall in love with cooking?
Probably the day I was first allowed
to use the stove all by myself, and I
finally got to cook for the whole family.
Yes, I think that's exactly when.

Go for it, my parents said. With three little words,
my own pilot light ignited—just burst into flames.

Forks on the left, spoons on the right.
Knives here, water glasses there.
Napkins on your lap.
Try not to burn the bread.

It was the enormous feeling of having
accomplished something grand,
something so grown-up. Here's to the chef!

Everybody dig in.
A clean plate is a happy plate.
A quiet room is a hungry room.

That was the best part, the quiet. I figured
out that it meant they were really enjoying
it, that I'd done something right. Even if it
was just soup. Even if it was just lunch.

A hush falls over the crowd.
Happy diners speechless with satisfaction.

Silent but for the slurping.

Crispy Coleslaw Pancake

Inspired by my favorite dish at one of my favorite Charleston restaurants, Xiao Bao Biscuit, this crispy slaw pancake is like a Southern take on okonomiyaki (oh-koh-no-mee-YA-ki)—the savory cabbage pancakes that hail from Osaka, Japan. This recipe provides such a unique way to enjoy a bag of coleslaw mix, as the crunchy shredded veggies are bound together by a creamy, sweet potato–fortified batter. This is a great thing to serve as a healthy lunch (I often do) because it won't drag your energy down. It also makes a perfect canvas for whatever toppings you like or happen to have hanging around. Creamy on the inside and crispy on the outside— you may never look at coleslaw the same way again.

Makes 4 (5-inch) pancakes

1 sweet potato
½ cup plain Greek yogurt
¼ cup buttermilk
2 large eggs
2 tablespoons whole wheat flour
1 teaspoon garlic powder
1 teaspoon salt, plus more for topping
Freshly ground black pepper

1 (16-ounce) bag coleslaw mix (or 16 ounces of finely shredded cabbage)
1 cup diced onion
1 tablespoon neutral cooking oil, such as grapeseed or canola, or ghee
Fried, poached, soft boiled eggs, sliced cucumbers, Comeback Sauce (page 22), and/or hot sauce, for serving

Cover 2 large baking sheets with parchment paper.

Pierce the sweet potato 4 to 5 times with a fork. Microwave for 5 to 6 minutes, or until very tender and easily pierced with a knife all the way through. Peel and put it in a medium mixing bowl. Mash it until it's as smooth as you can get it.

To the sweet potato, whisk in the yogurt, buttermilk, eggs, flour, garlic powder, salt, and lots of pepper.

In a large bowl, mix the coleslaw and onion together. Pour the sweet potato mixture into the coleslaw mixture and toss (I use my hands) until everything is very well blended.

Divide the slaw mixture evenly between the prepared baking sheets, forming and shaping it into 5-inch flat disks (about ¾ inch tall). Bake until deeply golden brown and crisped, 30 to 35 minutes.

Transfer the cooked pancakes to serving plates. Or just keep things rustic and top and serve them right on the baking sheet. Enjoy the pancakes while they're warm, served with eggs, cucumbers, comeback sauce, and/or hot sauce. Leftovers will keep for a few days in the refrigerator.

Sticky, Crispy Tofu with Maple Molasses Sauce

This recipe has one foot firmly planted in the South while the other is wandering around somewhere in Southeast Asia. Mimicking the wonderfully flavorful caramel fish and chicken dishes I love so much in Vietnamese cooking, I've adapted a similar notion in this lighter, slightly spicy, entirely plant-based version. We'll swap low-calorie tofu in as the protein of choice, and since we're using a nonstick skillet, we need to use only a small amount of oil to get it really crispy. Molasses and maple syrup help us nail a deep, caramel-like flavor without any refined sugar. I love this for lunch, as it satisfies my cravings for crunchy, salty fried foods (trademarks of Southern cooking) with no guilt.

Makes 2 to 4 servings

1 (16-ounce) block super-firm tofu
2 tablespoons neutral cooking oil, such as grapeseed or canola
¼ cup soy sauce (or tamari for gluten-free)
1 tablespoon molasses
1 tablespoon maple syrup
1 tablespoon buffalo-style hot sauce
⅓ cup water
Chopped scallion greens, for garnishing
Sesame seeds, for garnishing

Place the tofu on a plate and set a heavy-ish object on top of it, like a heavy plate or pan—just be careful not to break the tofu. This will push the excess water out, helping achieve that crispy texture we're going for. Let it sit for 20 minutes, and then drain off the excess water.

Cut the tofu into ¼- to ½-inch-thick planks or slices. Pour the oil into a large nonstick skillet set over medium-high heat. When it's hot, carefully place the tofu slices in the pan and cook until browned and crispy, 4 to 5 minutes per side. Transfer to a paper towel–lined plate to drain excess oil.

Drain and wipe out the oil from the pan and return it to the stovetop. Reduce the heat to medium. In a small bowl, stir together the soy sauce, molasses, maple syrup, and buffalo sauce. Add this to the skillet, along with the water. Let this simmer and reduce for 3 to 4 minutes.

Carefully place the tofu back in the pan and let it soak up the sauce (turn it over once or twice to help with this). Transfer to a serving plate and pour the pan sauce all over the top. Garnish with chopped scallions and sesame seeds.

Energizing Pecan Pie Bites

Pecan pie lovers will find a healthier happy place with these. It never ceases to amaze me how effectively pitted dates can help mimic the sweetness and texture of so many different desserts. Their natural creaminess and caramel-esque flavor are perfectly suited for a lighter riff on pecan pie. In this case, we'll create satisfying, two-bite "pies" that consist of only a few simple ingredients. Of course, these would fit nicely in the desserts chapter, but I love them as a midday pick-me-up with a glass of iced coffee or tea.

Makes about 30 (1-inch) pieces

4 cups raw pecan halves
4 cups pitted dates
2 teaspoons vanilla extract
¼ teaspoon salt

Put the pecans in a large skillet set over medium heat. Stirring occasionally, toast the pecans for 3 to 4 minutes, or until they're visibly beginning to darken and you can just smell them.

Transfer the toasted pecans to a food processor along with the dates, vanilla, and salt. Process until the ingredients are broken down and have combined into a homogeneous mixture that is not unlike a cookie dough. If your dates are struggling to smooth out (they might be older or dry), you can throw them in a small pot of boiling water and let them soak for 10 minutes, drain, and then carry on with the processing of it all.

Roll the mixture into 1- to 1½-inch balls. These will keep in a covered container for up to a week.

Note *Try adding in ⅔ cup of mini semisweet chocolate chips and/or 2 to 3 teaspoons of bourbon for other flavor combinations.*

Velvety Red Pepper and Tomato Soup

*A bowl to warm your bones
and bring a sense of calm to
your days, this simple tomato
and red pepper soup is as cozy
and comforting as the feeling
of a cool hand pressed against
your forehead when you're a
bit under the weather. It also
gets better the longer it sits—a
very attractive quality in,
well, anything? If you squint,
you can see the edges of a red
velvet cake in the ingredients
here, and though that was
unintentional when I wrote
this recipe, it is how the soup
got its cheeky name. A splash
of tangy buttermilk, some
cocoa and vinegar, and, of
course, a bright, vermillion
hue, draw a resemblance to the
South's beloved cake—though
in a very different, savory way.*

Makes 2 to 4 servings

1 tablespoon olive oil
1 cup diced sweet onion
1 (12-ounce) jar roasted red
   peppers, drained and diced
1 (6-ounce) can tomato paste
2 garlic cloves, minced
   or grated
1 teaspoon unsweetened
   cocoa powder
1 tablespoon coconut sugar
2 teaspoons vegetable stock
   concentrate or chicken
   stock concentrate
Salt
Freshly ground black pepper
2 tablespoons balsamic vinegar
1 to 2 cups vegetable
   or chicken stock
½ cup buttermilk (or
   coconut milk, for vegan)
1 (28-ounce) can
   crushed tomatoes

Pour the oil into a large pot set over medium heat. When it's hot,
add the onion and red peppers. Cook until the onion is tender,
about 5 minutes. Add the tomato paste, garlic, cocoa, coconut
sugar, stock concentrate, and a little salt and black pepper to
taste. Cook for 30 seconds more.

Add the vinegar, 1 cup of the stock, the buttermilk, and
tomatoes and stir to combine. Season to taste with salt and
pepper. Feel free to add more buttermilk to taste, too. Transfer
to a blender, or use an immersion blender, and purée until
totally smooth. Return to and reheat in the pot. If you think it
needs a little more stock, feel free to add the extra cup now. Stir
to combine.

Let the soup cool to room temperature and store in the
refrigerator, covered, for up to 4 days. It will freeze well for
about 1 month.

Note *Serve with Crunchy Black-Eyed Peas (page 121) or a salad
of watercress or arugula tossed in a little olive oil and fresh lemon
juice to make a light meal.*

Jammy Mignonette-Marinated Eggs

To me, a soft-boiled egg is one of the most enjoyable, simply perfect forms of healthy protein out there. A jammy, saucy center encased by just-cooked whites—it's a very satisfying arrangement all around, and I'm always seeking new ways to serve them. Enter this colorful, tangy, marinated crew. These are a bit like those Southern-style pickled eggs you'll see in delis and country stores, the white orbs suspended in vinegary, pink liquid. Here, though, there's lots of garlic and luscious olive oil going on, and the shallots and black pepper give a heady nod to the oyster's best friend, mignonette. These make a great breakfast or brunch option but are also an easily portable picnic snack or an impressive appetizer. Incredible? Yes. Edible? Also yes.

Makes 6 to 8 servings

8 large eggs
1 cup distilled white vinegar or red wine vinegar
¼ cup olive oil
1 teaspoon salt
½ teaspoon freshly ground black pepper
1 garlic clove, minced or grated
2 shallots, minced
Juice from 1 (14.5-ounce) can beets (save the beets for a salad or for snacking)
Finely chopped smoked almonds, for serving
Flaky sea salt, for serving (optional)

Fill a large pot three-fourths full of water and bring to a boil over high heat. When it's boiling, very carefully add the eggs. Boil for exactly 6 minutes (no longer) and transfer to a bowl of ice water. When cool enough to handle, peel the eggs.

Meanwhile, in a large bowl, whisk together the vinegar, oil, salt, pepper, garlic, shallots, and beet juice. Put the peeled eggs in this pickling mixture and let them marinate for at least 1 hour before slicing in half lengthwise.

To serve these, arrange the sliced eggs on a plate or platter and spoon a little of the pickling liquid all over them. Sprinkle some chopped smoked almonds on top and, if they need it, just a pinch of flaky sea salt.

These eggs will keep, covered, unsliced, and in the marinade in the fridge for up to 2 weeks. The marinade will keep for future uses as well, for up to several weeks. It makes a great dressing or sauce for vegetables of all shapes and sizes.

Butter-Bean Succotash

This recipe really could hang out in most of the chapters in this book, save for maybe desserts. I absolutely love this stuff—I snack on it and enjoy it for lunch in salads and on flatbread. It's wonderful in a wrap or even blended into a soup with some vegetable stock. Add this to some crispy roasted potatoes or some cooked whole wheat pasta for a great potato or pasta salad. In sum, succotash wins the congeniality award by a landslide—it's never not perfectly suited for any table, any occasion. In this version, we're using dramatically oversize butter beans, sweet corn, and cherry tomatoes. The whole lot will be swimming in a garlicky, olive oil–slicked buttermilk bath, which sounds pretty decadent, but it's not. This is the sort of deceptive trickery that makes for the best kind of light eating, I think.

Makes 4 to 6 servings

2 cups fresh corn kernels
1 cup halved cherry tomatoes
1 (15-ounce) can large butter
   beans, rinsed and drained
1 garlic clove, minced or grated
Salt
Freshly ground black pepper

¾ cup buttermilk
1 tablespoon olive oil
Chopped mixed fresh herbs
   for garnish (such as basil,
   dill, parsley, and chives)
Flaky sea salt, for topping

Put a large nonstick skillet over medium heat. Pour in the corn and tomatoes (no oil needed). Let them warm up and tenderize for about 5 minutes. Add the beans and garlic, season lightly with salt and pepper, and gently stir to mix everything together. Turn off the heat.

Pour the buttermilk into a large, deep bowl or on a serving plate. Drizzle the oil all over and season with salt and pepper. Top with the warm veggies and shower with fresh herbs. Sprinkle with flaky sea salt, if you've got it.

Frosted Mocha

This recipe is coming to you directly from Lucas, my husband. As a perfect midday pick-me-up or a whenever-you-feel-like-it moment of self-care, this drink is almost too good to be true. This fact is mostly attached to the low-cal, high-protein stats that the recipe sports. How is this not bad for me, you might wonder? It's okay—I went through a similar emotional journey myself the first time Lucas slid a tall glass of this across the counter to me. Not entirely unlike a very popular and somewhat iconic frosted fast-food treat, this one is built on healthy, simple ingredients and also has the very happy addition of coffee.

Makes 4 servings

4 cups ice
2 tablespoons cocoa powder
1 tablespoon stevia powder
⅓ cup almond milk
2 scoops chocolate whey protein powder
1 cup cold brew coffee, or to taste

In a blender, combine the ice, cocoa powder, stevia powder, almond milk, protein powder, and coffee. Blend on high until smooth and creamy, about 2 minutes.

Peaches with Basil-Whipped Cottage Cheese and Hot Sauce

I'm a sucker for hot sauce on fruit, and the cool basil and honey-scented whipped cheese makes for an ideal resting place for a pile of juicy sweet stone fruits. I eat this for lunch all the time. But why don't you just serve the peaches on top of regular cottage cheese and call it good? You may or may not be asking yourself this. My husband did, and it's a fair question. Peaches and cottage cheese have long been paired together and really, I'm just trying to breathe some new life into the ordinary, to shake things up (literally). This recipe messes around with the usual suspects, changing textures and flavors and producing what I'd like to think is a welcome refresh to a classic duo.

Makes 4 to 6 servings

16 ounces cottage cheese
2 tablespoons honey
½ cup loosely packed fresh basil leaves
Salt
Freshly ground black pepper
4 fresh ripe peaches or nectarines, sliced
Hot sauce, for topping (I like sriracha or green Tabasco)
Finely chopped toasted peanuts, for topping

In a food processor, combine the cottage cheese, honey, and basil and process until smooth. Season with salt and pepper to taste and spread onto a platter. Pile the peaches on top and sprinkle with hot sauce and chopped peanuts.

TEA LIGHTS

Maryanne invited me to a tea party once, many years ago. You've never been to one? It's time we fix that.

It was a marvelous, glittering affair, just for us. The dining room table was set with all of the best silver, my grandmother's prettiest china. Glimmers of gold, tiny hydrangea petals everywhere, plucked from the back garden. Spoons just for stirring the sugar.

It was lace and monograms and one lump or two? Can I have three? Is that too much? Of course, dah-ling, she'd say. There's no such thing.

With the radio's volume dial turned all the way to the right, she'd invite the crooners into the room, singing their glad old songs. You put those songs where it hurts, she'd say.

Shining trays of miniature sandwiches were passed around, their crusts nowhere in sight. Creamy Benedictine and pimiento cheese. Egg salad. Something called capers.

Sugar-struck and spinning like a top around the table, I'd dance from one edge of a song to the other, stopping to sip from my cup and nibble from this and that. Taking care not to ruin my dress.

Apple Tea Rose Tarts

Peanut butter sandwich crackers with apples on top: That's really all these are. But thanks to a very simple rolling method, and the help of some light and flaky phyllo dough, these mini apple rose tarts are so much more than the sum of their parts. I make a more decadent version of these, using buttery puff pastry and white sugar, but I think I actually like these more (it's the peanut butter, for me). Not only are they stunning, they're also healthy and work equally as a sweet party treat or a healthy after-school snack.

Makes 8 tarts

2 cups pomegranate juice
3 tablespoons apple or strawberry all-fruit spread
2 tablespoons honey
1 teaspoon vanilla bean paste or vanilla extract
2 large unpeeled apples, sliced into very thin half-moons (I use a mandoline for this)
Canola or vegetable oil, for brushing
8 peanut butter sandwich cookies or peanut butter crackers
8 sheets phyllo dough, thawed
¼ cup coconut sugar, plus more as needed
Powdered sugar, for dusting

Pour the pomegranate juice into a small saucepan over medium heat and add the fruit spread and honey. Simmer for 6 to 8 minutes, until everything is smooth and melted. Turn off the heat and add the vanilla.

Put the apple slices into a large bowl or baking pan and pour the hot syrupy mixture over top, ensuring all of the apples are covered. Let the apples soak for at least 30 minutes, to stain and soften.

Preheat the oven to 350°F. Adjust the rack to the middle position.

Meanwhile, brush each of 8 muffin cups with a little oil. Put a sandwich cookie in each of the greased muffin cups. Alternatively, you can crush the cookies in a plastic bag and press a tablespoon or so of the crumbly mixture down into the bottom of each cup. It works great either way.

Working on a clean, flat surface, lay a sheet of phyllo dough in front of you, the long edge closest to you. Brush the surface with a little oil, then lay a second sheet of phyllo on top. Repeat until 4 sheets are stacked and coated. Do the same thing again, creating a second 4-sheet-thick stack.

Using a sharp knife, cut each stack into 1-inch-wide strips (slicing from top to bottom, not across the stacks).

When the apple slices are pliable, arrange them horizontally in (slightly) overlapping rows down the length of each phyllo strip. I usually allot 6 to 8 apple slices per phyllo strip.

Starting at the ends closest to you, gently roll the strips up from end to end. Using a sharp knife, cut each roll in half. Place 4 halves into each of the prepared muffin cups, on top of the cookies (just gently squeeze them in place to fit snugly). The finished products will resemble small tea roses, but by no means need to all be perfect or exactly alike.

Sprinkle the tarts with the coconut sugar and bake for 22 to 24 minutes, until bubbling and just barely golden around the tips and edges. Cool for at least 10 minutes, dust with powdered sugar, and carefully remove them with a knife or inverted spatula.

Honeyed Vanilla-Watermelon Tea

The best way to sweeten tea, in my opinion, is with tons of fresh, juicy watermelon. I've always enjoyed Mexican-style watermelon aguas frescas, and here, I'm merging that simply beautiful beverage with some freshly steeped tea, sweet vanilla, and lots of fresh mint. We'll nix the sugar with which sweet tea is typically loaded and instead sweeten this drink with a touch of golden honey. I can't think of a better pick-me-up on a hot day than this subtly flavored, icy refresher.

Makes about 6 cups

4 cups water
4 tea bags (ginger, black, Earl Grey, and vanilla chamomile are my favorites)
¼ cup honey
5 cups (1-inch cubes) seedless watermelon, plus more if desired
2 teaspoons vanilla bean paste or vanilla extract
1 cup fresh mint leaves

In a small saucepan or pot set over high heat, bring the water to a boil. Once it's boiling, turn off the heat. Add the teabags to the water, along with the honey. Stir to melt the honey into the tea, and allow things to steep and cool until the tea has fallen closer to room temperature; it takes about 25 minutes (you can speed this up by popping the tea in the refrigerator or freezer).

When the tea has cooled, remove the tea bags and pour it into a blender along with the cubes of watermelon and the vanilla. Blend on high speed until the melon is totally broken down and smooth. Feel free to add more watermelon if you like for a little more texture and body. Pour the watermelon tea into a pitcher and add the mint. The mint flavor will subtly infuse the tea as it sits.

Serve in glasses filled with ice. Secret Garden Ice (page 94) is especially beautiful here.

Secret Garden Ice

Alive with locals and curious travelers, the streets of downtown Charleston are dripping with history and a distinctly Southern sort of charm. Camera in tow, I often wander around down south of Broad Street, purposefully allowing the Holy City's maze of scrawny alleyways and backstreets to swallow me up in their wild beauty. It's the kind of beauty that takes its time, and it shape-shifts depending on where the sun hangs in the sky. From the bustling main drags to the darkened, narrow tributaries that flow all around, these streets hold many secrets.

It's the gardens that get me, though, every time. Tucked in and all around the stone and brick are dozens of lush, impeccably well-kept gardens, their quiet serenade a joy to stumble upon. Notes of jasmine, honeysuckle, and wild berries perfume the air, their heady scent just floating all around like it's no big deal. This is my favorite Charleston, the parts that show themselves in moments unexpected, letting you in on just a little bit of their mystery.

Hands wrapped around wrought-iron gates, my daughter peers into these gardens and swears there are mystical fairies all around, making their homes among the flower petals, lily pads, and cool, falling waters of the many fountains.

It's the most delicious thing, and we drink it all in, sipping from it slowly, a little at a time. Maps aren't allowed, of course. They'd ruin things—unbind the spell. The fun, after all, is in the not knowing. It's about stopping and smelling the roses, both literal and otherwise. It's about finding your own way for just a pretty little while.

This entry is more of an idea than a recipe, an ode to the secret Southern gardens we love so much. I've found that there is no one who isn't charmed by this stunning, glistening botanical ice. Edible flowers and sweet berries are suspended in cubes of frozen tea, and they gently stain the waters, lemonades, and all other manner of beverages that receive them—that extra special touch. This ice is especially lovely in the Honeyed Vanilla-Watermelon Tea (page 93).

The fun with these frozen floral jewels is in creating something all your own. No maps allowed.

Use as much or as little of any tea you like; that part is up to you. Use dried berries or fresh, use any shape of ice cube you enjoy or have on hand. Here's what you see in the photograph, but I never make these the same way twice.

Half of the ice is passion fruit plus hibiscus tea, and the other half is classic Southern sweet tea, both store-bought. I drop a few edible flowers into each ice cube slot along with 5 or 6 wild blueberries and then fill to the top with tea. Freeze solid and then use anywhere and everywhere.

Jalapeño Popper Quiche Bites

I'm not sure if the quiche is elevating the humble jalapeño popper or if it's the other way around, but I do know that the spicy-ish, creamy, garlicky flavors running through this recipe are enough to keep anyone coming back for more. The quiche is a classic teatime sort of dish, and while I do love them so, the traditional versions you most often see are incredibly rich—almost unbelievably so. Here, we're stripping away some of the heavier elements (okay, all of them) while still maintaining all of the flavor. A not-so-small victory! Cottage cheese, yogurt, lots of pickled jalapeños, and smoky almonds work together in one very tasty, and very low-cal, low-carb dish.

Makes 4 to 6 servings

Natural nonstick cooking spray
¾ cup finely chopped
  smoked almonds
2 teaspoons olive oil
1 cup pickled jalapeño slices
1 cup chopped sweet onion
Salt
Freshly ground black pepper
2 large garlic cloves,
  minced or grated
4 whole large eggs plus
  8 whites, beaten
⅓ cup plain Greek yogurt
⅓ cup cottage cheese
2 ounces goat cheese

Preheat the oven to 375°F. Adjust the rack to the middle position. Lightly spray a 9-inch pie plate with a cooking spray. Scatter the chopped almonds evenly across the plate (you can use more, if you like).

Pour the oil into a large nonstick skillet set over medium heat. When it's hot, add the jalapeños and onion. Season lightly with salt and pepper. Cook, stirring, for 4 to 5 minutes, just to tenderize the onion. Add the garlic and cook for 30 seconds more.

Season the eggs lightly with salt and pepper. Stir in the cooked vegetable mixture, along with the yogurt and cottage cheese. Pour the mixture into the pie plate, filling just below the top. Pinch off bits of the goat cheese and scatter them over the quiche mixture.

Bake until puffed and golden and done in the center, about 30 minutes. This will keep, covered, in the refrigerator for up to 4 days and will freeze nicely for up to 2 months.

Smoked Salmon and Cucumber Tea Sandwiches

Five ingredients and five minutes of prep time. That's all you need to whip up these incredibly simple yet delicious bites. The bread you most often see in tea sandwiches has fallen away, as I find the cucumber itself makes a perfectly good house for the salmon and creamy filling. You can, of course, mix together any manner of savory, creamy, cheesy fillings for these. But in the name of convenience and efficiency, I just reach for something that's already mixed, already done for me. We'll call it my "tea party trick." How does she do it? Use as much or as little of each component as you like and watch them vanish, one by one. They're so crunchy and addictive, you'll never miss the bread.

Makes 12 to 14 sandwiches

Garlic and herb cheese spread, such as Boursin or Alouette
1 English cucumber, sliced into ¼-inch slices
4 ounces smoked salmon
⅔ cup chopped fresh dill
Toasted sesame seeds and poppy seeds, for sprinkling

Spread some of the cheese spread onto 1 side of each cucumber slice (you could also pipe it, if you want to be fancy). Top with a little bit of smoked salmon (cut and slice it into portions as needed to fit) and some chopped dill. Top with another cucumber slice. Sprinkle some of the sesame and poppy seeds on the tops of each little sandwich and serve chilled.

Cobbled Stone Fruit and Melon Salad

Syrupy, honey-scented tea. Hints of sweet vanilla and mint. A riot of vibrant, warmly hued fruit. These are the simple, unassuming building blocks of this recipe. The whole point here, really, is to coax out the best flavors that the fruit has to offer. The sticky, jammy marinade will soak into the cut fruit—the peaches and plums, honeydew and watermelon—sweetening it, turning its volume up a little bit. You'll wind up with this beautiful, shimmering mess of fruit that, even when it's not in peak season, will still taste pretty magical.

Makes 6 cups

2 pounds (6 to 8 fruits) mixed stone fruits, such as peaches, plums, and nectarines

5 cups cubed mixed melon, such as honeydew, cantaloupe, and watermelon

1 cup water

1 ginger or Earl Grey tea bag

⅓ cup honey

2 tablespoons peach or apricot all-fruit spread

1 tablespoon balsamic vinegar

1 teaspoon vanilla bean paste or vanilla extract

⅓ cup fresh mint leaves

Peel, seed, and cut the stone fruits into bite-size pieces. Arrange with the melon on a big platter.

In a small saucepan set over medium heat, combine the water, tea bag, and honey. Bring to a boil and then reduce to a simmer. Add the fruit spread and vinegar, stirring to melt into the sauce. Let this mixture reduce for about 5 minutes, until it has thickened and coats the back of a spoon. Turn off the heat and stir in the vanilla and the mint. Pour this warm marinade over the fruit, taking your time to really soak each bit.

Let the fruit sit for at least 10 minutes before serving. This is great either at room temperature or refrigerated. It will keep covered in the fridge for up to 3 days.

Black Tea and Bay- Braised Alliums on Toast

They say if you love something to let it go, and if it comes back to you, it was yours all along. This essentially sums up my relationship with bread. I said goodbye to it at one point, hitching my dietary preferences to a fad or trend that didn't fit me so well. I've amended things now, having learned that simply reducing the amount I eat is a far better tactic than cutting it out altogether. I'm simply not going to not eat bread, but I do look for ways to limit my consumption of it because this serves me better. As such, the fancified toast craze that has been sweeping the globe for a while now has my name written all over it. Less bread, more healthy toppings—I like this. Here, we'll explore the floral, fragrant qualities of both bay leaves and tea and how they transform a heap of oniony, garlicky things into a topping that is otherworldly delicious.

Makes 6 to 8 servings

6 cups (give or take) mixed alliums: roughly chopped/sliced onions, roughly chopped ramps (if and when you can get them—do!), scallion whites, whole garlic cloves, pearl onions, sliced leeks, etc.
16 to 20 fresh bay leaves (1 package)
1 lemon, sliced
Salt
Freshly ground black pepper
3 cups chicken or vegetable stock
1 tablespoon sherry vinegar or apple cider vinegar
3 black tea bags
6 to 8 slices favorite whole-grain bread, toasted
Flaky sea salt, for sprinkling

Preheat the oven to 325°F. Adjust the rack to the middle position.

Spread the various alliums evenly in a large baking dish. Top with the bay leaves and lemon slices. Season lightly with salt and pepper.

In a saucepan over medium-high heat, combine the stock, vinegar, and tea bags. Bring to a boil, turn off the heat, and let the mixture steep for 10 minutes. Pour the infused stock all around the dish, just until the liquid reaches about halfway up the sides of the vegetables.

Oven-braise the vegetables until they are very tender, 35 to 40 minutes.

Remove the bay leaves and serve the tender vegetables on top of the toasted bread, with a little of the braising liquid poured over top (this now necessitates a fork). Sprinkle with flaky sea salt.

Note *These make a great side dish or topping for roasted or grilled proteins (steak, chicken, seafood, etc.).*

Butter Bean, Butternut, and Buttermilk Salad in Butter Lettuce

The most buttery recipe in this book doesn't actually have a trace of butter anywhere in sight. This is my vegetarian answer to the very heavy, mayonnaise-packed "salads" that are ubiquitous when it comes to simple Southern entertaining—classic tea party fare to be sure. But the dressing is just garlicky yogurt and tahini, with some lemon and buttermilk for smoothness (sorry, mayo). The combination of meaty butter beans, sweet squash, and buttery avocado is delicious and so good for you.

Piled up in butter lettuce leaves as handheld "wraps" or enjoyed on top of the crunchy lettuce with a fork, this buttery salad will leave you feeling healthfully satisfied.

Makes about 3 cups

1 to 2 teaspoons olive oil
1 (15-ounce) package frozen cubed butternut squash, thawed
Salt
Freshly ground black pepper
1 (15-ounce) can butter beans, drained and rinsed
2 ripe avocados, diced
1 shallot, minced
¼ cup tahini
¾ cup plain Greek yogurt
¼ cup buttermilk
Juice of ½ lemon
½ teaspoon garlic powder
1 head butter lettuce, leaves separated

Pour the oil into a large nonstick skillet set over medium heat. When it's hot, add the squash and cook, undisturbed, until it begins to char and brown. Season lightly with salt and pepper. Flip the squash and cook on the other side, 6 to 8 minutes total. Transfer the squash to a large mixing bowl. Add the butter beans, avocados, and shallot. Gently toss to mix.

In a small bowl, combine the tahini, yogurt, buttermilk, lemon juice, and garlic powder. Taste and season with salt and pepper. This recipe really needs a good amount of salt to be its best, so don't be shy!

Pour your desired amount of dressing over the veggie mixture and gently toss to coat everything. Serve wrap style with butter lettuce leaves on the side, or you can arrange the lettuce on plates and pile the salad on top. Serve with any leftover dressing on the side.

Honey and Lemon–Soaked Teacup Cakes

With no refined sugar or butter, these tea cakes are so much healthier than a classic version, but they're truly just as delicious. I bake these in muffin pans, but you could pour the batter into a standard cake pan and bake for about 30 minutes, or until a tester comes out clean, if you prefer. A mixture of superfine almond flour and soft cake flour makes the perfect crumb, and a wholesome combination of buttermilk, coconut oil, and olive oil builds moisture.

The lemony, honey-laced syrup gets brushed all over the warm cakes, making the need for any other topping or flourish totally unnecessary.

Makes 12 teacakes

Natural nonstick cooking spray
1 cup superfine almond flour
1 cup cake flour
2 ½ teaspoons baking powder
1 teaspoon baking soda
¼ teaspoon salt
⅓ cup melted coconut oil
⅓ cup olive oil
Zest and juice of 1 large lemon
4 teaspoons vanilla extract, divided
3 large eggs
¾ cup full-fat buttermilk
¾ cup honey

Preheat the oven to 350°F. Adjust the oven rack to the middle position. Spray each of 12 muffin cups with cooking spray and place on a large baking sheet (this will catch any sneaky spillage).

In a mixing bowl, whisk together the almond flour, cake flour, baking powder, baking soda, and salt; set aside.

Add the oils, lemon zest, and 2 teaspoons of the vanilla to the bowl of a stand mixer or to a large mixing bowl using a handheld mixer. Add the eggs, 1 at a time, mixing until each is blended.

Add about one-third of the flour mixture (just eyeball it) to the egg mixture and mix until combined. Add half of the buttermilk and mix until just combined. Add another ⅓ of the flour mixture and repeat until everything has been added.

Fill the prepared muffin cups two-thirds of the way full with the batter. Bake for 25 to 27 minutes, or until deeply golden and a tester inserted in the centers comes out clean. Let the cakes cool for 6 to 8 minutes, then transfer them to a wire rack set over a baking sheet, bottoms facing up (we will brush/soak them upside down for maximum absorption).

Meanwhile, in a small saucepan over medium heat, combine the honey, lemon juice, and remaining 2 teaspoons of vanilla. Simmer gently for about 5 minutes, then remove from the heat. Using a pastry brush (preferably), brush the syrup all over the warm cakes. I usually brush once, let it soak in for a few minutes, and then brush on another layer.

These will keep, covered, in a cool dry place for up to 4 days. I like to serve them upside down, draped in a heap of Yogurty Whipped Cream (page 21).

Not Your Mama's Ambrosia

*If you squint, can you see the
ambrosia in here? Inspired
by the almost sickly sweet
classic Southern "salad," my
riff is fresher and just a little
more interesting, all around.
We have the olives to thank
for that and the use of clean,
whole ingredients. That said,
feel free to omit the olives if
you just can't even. We will
touch all ends of the flavor
and texture spectrums here,
and as a person who writes
recipes, there are few things
that make me happier.*

Makes 6 servings

1 (15-ounce) can coconut
  cream, refrigerated
Salt
Freshly ground black pepper
½ cup raw pecan pieces
½ cup unsweetened
  coconut flakes
1 fresh pineapple, peeled, cored
  and sliced into ½-inch rings
3 mandarin oranges, peeled
  and separated into segments
1 (15-ounce) can pitted whole
  buttery black or green olives,
  drained (optional, I suppose)
½ cup dried cherries
Honey, for drizzling
Flaky sea salt, for sprinkling

Taking care not to shake or invert the can, open the coconut cream and scoop off the solidified cream on top, leaving the liquid behind and/or saving for another use (smoothies, iced tea, lemonade, etc.). Spoon the coconut cream into a bowl and whisk to soften it. Season with salt and pepper to taste and spread on a plate or platter.

In a large, dry skillet set over medium heat, toast the pecans and coconut, stirring frequently, until fragrant and lightly browned, 5 to 7 minutes.

Top the coconut cream with the pineapple rings, mandarin segments, and olives (if using, but I really recommend you use them). Sprinkle the toasted coconut and pecans over top, and finish with the dried cherries, a generous drizzle of honey, and a sprinkle of flaky sea salt.

BREAK LIGHTS

"Snack" is such a funny word.

*These little bites and bits of things we sneak
to break up our days.*

*Maybe no one's watching.
Maybe everyone is.*

*Maybe you only have one minute
Maybe you have a hundred of them.
It's important all the same.*

So pull over. Pull up a chair.

Sit down. Slow down.

Steal away.

*Grab hold of the small, fleeting moments
that fight against the rising
tides of our busy lives.*

Take a break. Take a breath.

*Before the light turns green
and away you go again.*

Salty, Seedy Crackers

When I say that these are among the easiest homemade crackers around, I mean that completely. We're just going to shower some flaky-as-hell phyllo dough (I'm using it again!) with sesame seeds, sea salt, and some garlic and onion powder. This is a nice way to use the ground, dried spices that are relegated to the shadowy corners of your spice drawer. Garlic powder, in particular, is sort of scoffed at and ridiculed, bless its heart. It has its place, though, since the fresh stuff runs the risk of burning at times. That place would be right here, atop a bunch of shatteringly crisp, toasty homemade crackers.

Makes about 48
(2-inch) crackers

6 sheets phyllo dough
Olive oil, for brushing
1 egg white, beaten
Flaky sea salt, for sprinkling
2 tablespoons black
   sesame seeds
2 tablespoons white sesame
   seeds or benne seeds
   (if you can get them)
1 teaspoon garlic powder
1 teaspoon onion powder

Preheat the oven to 350°F. Adjust the rack to the middle position. Line 2 baking sheets with parchment paper.

Lay a piece of phyllo on the first prepared baking sheet and brush gently and evenly with the oil. Top with a second phyllo sheet and coat again in oil. Top with a third sheet and brush with a thin, even layer of the egg white. Using the second prepared baking sheet, repeat these steps with the 3 remaining phyllo sheets.

Sprinkle each phyllo stack evenly with some sea salt followed by the black and white sesame seeds and garlic and onion powders. You want to evenly distribute the seeds and seasonings between the 2 stacks.

Using a pizza cutter or a sharp knife, cut the sheets into 2-inch crackers (or any size you want). To get them to separate nicely, go back over your cuts again—this will ensure they break and bake apart from each other.

Bake until golden brown, 3½ to 4½ minutes. Let them cool a bit before handling. These will keep in a covered container in a cool, dry place for up to 5 days.

Note *I enjoy these crackers served with Caramelized Onion and Pimiento Slather (page 23). So tasty!*

Figs in a Blanket

Nothing says "party" quite like food on a toothpick. And to me, nothing says "delicious" quite like the sweet-savory combo of salty pork and luscious, creamy fruit. You'll see figs and peaches wrapped up in thin slices of salty country or honey-baked ham on appetizer platters all up and down the South. It is very much a thing. Although they are often stuffed with rich cheeses and whatnot, I'm sticking with the simpler version—sticky honey, creamy figs, and thin-sliced ham. The hot honey acts as a glue for the ham and figs, but even so, I recommend using toothpicks to secure everything. These are nothing less than decadent and always tend to disappear really fast.

Makes 8 to 10 servings
as an appetizer

10 to 12 ripe figs, halved lengthwise
3 tablespoons store-bought hot honey
Flaky sea salt, for sprinkling
Freshly ground black pepper
4 to 6 thin country ham slices or prosciutto

Preheat the oven to 375°F. Adjust the rack to the middle position and line a baking sheet with a piece of parchment paper or a silicone baking mat.

Brush each fig half with some of the honey, coating them all over. Sprinkle each with a pinch of flaky sea salt and some pepper to taste.

Cut the ham slices in half lengthwise and wrap or roll these slices around the figs as best you can (this in no way needs to look or be perfect). You can even cut the ham slices again, if you want to stretch them further. Up to you! Secure each fig and its blanket with a toothpick and arrange them on the prepared baking sheet.

Bake for 8 to 10 minutes, or until the ham has just browned and crisped a little. These are best warm, but they're still nice at room temperature.

Red Velvet Pecans

Reminiscent of the candy-coated sugar shacks one might find on a walk through the Historic Charleston City Market (a favorite family stroll of ours), these pecans are something else. Though they sport a gorgeously crimson hue and boast a satisfying, crackling crust, it's actually what they don't have that is most attractive: no refined sugar. No butter. These sweet treats are made with just maple syrup, cocoa, cinnamon, vanilla, and a simple-yet-effective method that coaxes out the best parts of a classic glazed pecan without the guilt. I like to serve these with cocktails or as a very special salad topper around the holidays.

Makes 3 cups

3 cups raw pecan halves
½ cup pure maple syrup
½ teaspoon ground cinnamon
2 teaspoons unsweetened cocoa powder
2 teaspoons vanilla extract
1 (1-ounce) bottle red food coloring
Salt

Preheat the oven to 325°F. Adjust the rack to the middle position. Line a large baking sheet with parchment paper or a silicone baking mat.

In a mixing bowl, toss together the pecans, maple syrup, cinnamon, cocoa, vanilla, and as much red food coloring as you see fit (I use almost a whole bottle to really get them nice and red, but it's up to you). Season with a pinch of salt. Pour the mixture onto the baking sheet and spread into a single layer. The maple syrup will pool around the nuts a bit—this is okay.

Roast for 10 minutes. Stir the pecans and put them back in the oven. Continue stirring them every 5 minutes until they have roasted for about 25 minutes. They will continue to crisp up as they cool. Cool them completely before transferring to a lidded container. These will keep for up to 1 week.

Crushed Corn Veggie Dip

I stumbled across Chef Sohla El-Waylly's wildly clever savory Fun Dip idea while on a hungry internet recipe search, and my veggies have been better for it ever since. This is the greatest way to get people to eat their vegetables, and you can have fun with the flavors, adding a little of this and that to suit your tastes. This corn-forward combo is crunchy and salty and plays well with so many things. While I use it primarily as a dry dip for raw veggies, it's also amazing as a soup and salad topper (in place of breadcrumbs), and as a coating for corn on the cob.

Makes about 1½ cups

1½ cups corn nuts
1 teaspoon nutritional yeast
⅓ cup smoked almonds, chopped
1 teaspoon garlic powder
1 teaspoon onion powder
Sliced fresh vegetables, for dipping (carrots, radishes, cucumber, and/ or summer squash)

In a food processor, pulse the corn nuts, nutritional yeast, almonds, garlic powder, and onion powder until finely ground and powdery (it's loud, I apologize). Pour into a bowl and serve with sliced veggies just as you would a creamy vegetable dip. It will cling to the moisture in most vegetables, making for a savory, crunchy coating.

This will keep in a covered container in a cool, dry place for up to 2 weeks.

Note *This also works beautifully on grilled or boiled corn on the cob.*

Chicken-Fried Popcorn

Don't let the name fool you—this stuff isn't what you think. It's nothing like popcorn chicken, and it's a far cry from the massively rich tubs of butter-drenched popcorn that I used to stuff my face with as a kid. Instead, this is some freshly popped corn tossed and toasted in a hot skillet with a feisty collective of flavor agents that do some serious work on these kernels. I got the idea from Australian chicken fries/chips, which feature an umami bomb of a seasoning called "chicken salt." Here, we'll make our own version using bouillon, fresh garlic, and some dried seasonings that, when activated in a little bit of ghee and olive oil, become popcorn's best secret weapon (my apologies to movie theater butter).

Makes about 12 cups

FOR THE POPCORN
Grapeseed, avocado oil, or ghee, for cooking

½ cup popcorn kernels

FOR THE TOPPING
¼ cup olive oil, plus more as needed

2 tablespoons ghee, butter, or more olive oil

1 chicken bouillon cube or 2 teaspoons chicken stock concentrate

1 teaspoon poultry seasoning

1½ teaspoons (about 1 large clove) minced or grated fresh garlic

Salt

To make the popcorn: Pour a thin layer of cooking oil into the bottom of a large, deep, lidded pot set over medium to medium-high heat. Put 1 kernel of popcorn in the pot, cover with the lid, and wait for it to pop. When it has, add the rest of the kernels and close the lid. Cook for 3 to 4 minutes, until the kernels have (mostly) all popped.

Transfer the popped corn to a large mixing bowl and set aside.

To make the topping: In the same pot set over medium-low heat, combine the olive oil, ghee, bouillon, and poultry seasoning. Breaking up the bouillon cube as you go, stir-fry the flavorings in the oil for about 30 seconds. Add the garlic and cook for about 20 seconds more.

Reduce the heat to low, add the popcorn back to the pot, and toss with the flavored oil, allowing it to toast and "fry" gently; it takes about 1 minute. Just keep tossing so the popcorn really picks up the flavoring. Season with salt to taste and feel free to add more of any ingredient to suit your tastes. Serve right away.

Benedictine-ish

Born and raised a Kentucky girl, I grew up attending social gatherings where Benedictine spread was almost always present in all of its green, glowing glory. A Derby party just isn't complete without it. If you've never heard of it, it's essentially a cucumber dip held together with the not-so-light combination of mayo and cream cheese. A little onion and a drop of green food coloring complete the scene. But honestly? This is such a simple recipe to lighten up without sacrificing a bit of flavor or creamy goodness. Whipped cottage cheese, yogurt, and avocado contribute to the luscious texture and give a naturally green hue to this addicting dip that doubles as a great sandwich spread.

Makes about 1 ⅓ cups

⅔ cup plain Greek yogurt
⅔ cup cottage cheese
½ ripe avocado
Juice of ½ lemon, or more to taste
⅓ cup minced onion
⅔ cup grated cucumber, water squeezed or drained out
½ teaspoon salt
Cucumber slices, for garnish
Crackers, for serving

In a food processor or high-speed blender, combine the yogurt, cottage cheese, avocado, lemon juice, and onion and blend until smooth and creamy. Transfer the mixture to a bowl and fold in the drained cucumber. Season with the salt and refrigerate until needed. Garnish with cucumber slices and serve cold with crackers. This will keep in a covered container in the refrigerator for up to 3 days.

Note *This is also great slathered across a platter as a creamy anchor for a big pile of roasted vegetables.*

Grits and Honey Granola Bars

Healthier though they may be, these bear a close resemblance to the seemingly infinite amount of store-bought granola bars I consumed as a kid. Managing to be both tender and crunchy all at once, these bars really have a lot going for them. The addition of instant grits adds a fantastic popping crunch to the mix, and it helps to bind and bring everything together. If you're a honey lover like me, then these are the bars for you. I make a batch and then enjoy them as a midday or late-morning snack throughout the week.

Makes about 12 servings

Natural nonstick cooking spray
3 cups old-fashioned
   rolled oats
1 cup instant grits
   (yellow or white)
½ teaspoon salt
1 teaspoon baking soda
1 teaspoon ground cinnamon
½ cup coconut oil
½ cup honey, plus extra
   for drizzling
2 tablespoons coconut
   sugar or brown sugar
2 teaspoons vanilla extract

Preheat the oven to 350°F. Line a 9 x 13-inch baking dish with parchment paper or aluminum foil and spray liberally with cooking spray. Be sure to leave some of the parchment or foil hanging over the edges of the pan as easy-to-grab handles when you want to remove the bars.

In a large bowl, combine the oats, grits, salt, baking soda, and cinnamon; stir to mix very well. In a separate smaller bowl, combine the coconut oil and honey and microwave until the oil is totally melted, about 30 seconds or so. Add the coconut sugar and vanilla and stir to combine everything.

Pour the honey mixture into the oats mixture and stir until everything is well coated. Pour the mixture into the prepared pan. Use your measuring cup to press down on the surface of the granola bar mixture—this will help pack it all in and create the crunchy bars we're looking for (you can also use a glass for this—whatever works).

Bake for 15 minutes and then remove from the oven. Evenly drizzle the granola bar mixture with more honey, zig-zagging over the whole surface area (2 to 3 tablespoons). Bake for 6 to 8 more minutes, or just until you get a nice golden-brown color.

Cool for just 8 minutes, transfer to a cutting board or smooth surface, and then cut into bars. If you wait much longer than that, the bars will harden to the point where cutting will become pretty difficult. Let them cool completely after cutting before you store or eat them.

SPOTLIGHT

The terms "instant" and "quick-cooking" are often applied interchangeably to grits, and simply mean they have been precooked a bit. Instant grits are also more finely ground, so they cook faster and work in unique applications like these whereas regular grits would not (believe me, I tried).

Parmesan Baked Pickles with Remoulade Sauce

Let's hear it for the person who first thought to fry a pickle. Deep-fried pickles really are a thing of beauty, aren't they? They're hard not to love, especially when dunked into a creamy, cooling sauce of some sort. This version nixes the deep fryer and mayonnaise-based sauce for a much lighter squad of ingredients. Grated Parmesan cheese bakes onto dill pickle chips like it's meant to be—crunchy, golden brown, and perfectly salty. Remoulade sauce is one of my mom's favorite things, and this lighter version is just as tasty but far more dunkable, given its healthier status. This sauce also works as a great sandwich spread and salad dressing.

Makes 4 to 6 servings
as an appetizer

FOR THE PICKLES
1 (16-ounce) jar spicy dill pickle chips
6 ounces grated Parmesan cheese
Natural nonstick cooking spray

FOR THE REMOULADE SAUCE
¾ cup plain Greek or regular yogurt
¼ cup spicy Creole mustard or garlic mustard
1½ teaspoons Creole seasoning
1 to 2 teaspoons prepared horseradish
1 tablespoon Worcestershire sauce
1 tablespoon spicy pickle juice (from the jar)
½ teaspoon salt
¾ teaspoon garlic powder
Freshly ground black pepper
Hot sauce

To make the pickles: Preheat the oven to 375°F. Adjust the rack to the middle position. Line a large baking sheet with parchment paper or a silicone baking mat.

Dredge each pickle chip in the Parmesan cheese, pressing the cheese into both sides. Place on the prepared baking sheet in an even layer. Spray lightly with cooking spray and bake for 15 to 20 minutes, or until the cheese is golden brown.

To make the remoulade sauce: In a medium bowl, stir together the yogurt, mustard, Creole seasoning, horseradish, Worcestershire sauce, pickle juice, salt, garlic powder, plenty of pepper, and hot sauce to taste until smooth and blended. Serve with the warm baked pickles.

Pimiento Cheese Hummus

While pimiento cheese may have actually gotten its start in New York, it certainly found its wings in the South, as it is now a beloved and widely enjoyed item all across the region. With half the cheese of a traditional version and no mayo in sight, my light pimiento cheese hummus takes advantage of the roasted pimientos that are already incorporated into a store-bought red pepper hummus, making for a very quick and easy recipe. What's more, healthy and flavorful Greek yogurt gives this hummus a very creamy texture. Seedy, whole-grain crackers complete the scene as wholesome dippers—a far cry from the fried corn chips I grew up eating alongside my family's classic dip recipe.

Makes about 1½ cups

1 cup roasted red
   pepper hummus
4 ounces extra-sharp
   cheddar cheese
¼ cup plain Greek yogurt
¼ cup diced onion
1 teaspoon minced or
   grated garlic
½ teaspoon salt
Olive oil, for garnishing
   (optional)
Paprika, for
   garnishing (optional)
Seedy whole-grain
   crackers, for serving
Fresh veggies, for serving

In a food processor, combine the hummus, cheese, yogurt, onion, garlic, and salt. Process on high until very smooth and creamy. Transfer to a serving bowl and, if you like, top with a drizzle of olive oil and a sprinkle of paprika. Serve with crackers and veggies for dipping.

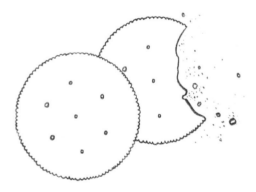

Crunchy Black-Eyed Peas

The once-famed deep-fried black-eyed peas from Relish restaurant in Roswell, Georgia, were brought to my attention by Alton Brown, who declared them one of the best things he'd ever eaten. I can confirm, after much "research," that fried black-eyed peas really are something else. But it turns out that you can achieve the same deeply satisfying crunch and crispy, salty, popping goodness by baking the peas instead. No deep-frying required. Great as both a midday or happy hour snack or as a soup and salad topper, these peas have so much more going on inside than meets the . . . um . . . eye. Just be sure to soak them overnight so they're ready to roll when you are.

Makes about 4 cups

16-ounces fresh black-eyed peas (not canned)
1 ¾ cups white distilled vinegar, divided
32 ounces vegetable stock
1 small onion, quartered
5 garlic cloves, smashed
1 teaspoon salt, plus more
1 tablespoon olive oil

At least 12 hours before cooking, put the black-eyed peas in a large mixing bowl and cover with water by an inch. Add ¾ cup of the vinegar. Let the peas soak, adding more water if needed.

After their 12-hour soak, drain and rinse the peas. Put them in a large pot over medium-high heat. Add the stock, quartered onion, garlic, and the remaining 1 cup of vinegar. Season with 1 teaspoon of salt and add water if necessary to fully cover the peas. Boil gently for 25 minutes, then drain.

Put a paper towel over a large baking sheet and pour the peas over the top, allowing the paper to absorb any excess water. Discard the paper towel and toss the peas (still on the baking sheet) with the olive oil and a generous sprinkling of salt (don't be shy—this is what makes them so good).

Bake about 30 minutes, until the peas are a deep, almond-butter brown, stirring every 6 to 8 minutes to help with even browning and to prevent sticking.

Cool almost completely before enjoying. These will keep in a covered container in the refrigerator for up to 5 days.

GREEN LIGHTS

When I dream of the South,
it's almost all in green.

Kudzu draped over the trees on
the side of the highway.

A willow's downward weeping,
ivy's upward creeping.

Moss hanging from gnarled, craggy
oaks, dramatic in its silent dripping.

Endless rolling fields, valleys, and hills.
The blue-green grasses of my childhood.

A sweet scent of mint escapes
from a julep's copper mug.
A sweet sentiment.

Sweet peas and string beans. Okra.
Collards. Ramps. Granny's apple peels.

Corn husks and leafy carrot tops.
Tomatoes fried at the Whistle Stop.

Technicolor dreams of unripened treasures
Lying in wait in Southern ground.

Spring breaks,
It cracks the world wide open,
Releasing the dormant, verdant wild.

Chili-Soaked Watermelon with Smoked Almonds

This is my lighter, more healthful take on one of the most popular recipes on my website, My Kitchen Little. I have a watermelon and mozzarella recipe that features a sinfully delicious hot candied bacon dressing. It's pretty incredible, yes, but I've found this lighter version to be just as satisfying. The spicy "soak" seeps into the sweet fruit and transforms it into something that just sings with flavor—it marinates it, essentially. Smoked almonds, in my opinion, are great on everything, but in this case, they perfectly replace the fatty bacon and offer a great crunch. To lighten things up even more, simply omit the mozzarella.

Makes 4 to 6 servings

2 tablespoons Asian-style chili sauce, such as sambal olek or sriracha (you can use less, if you prefer less heat)
2 tablespoons honey
1 teaspoon apple cider vinegar
¼ cup olive oil
Flaky sea salt, for sprinkling
Freshly ground black pepper
1 small seedless watermelon, sliced into wedges
8 ounces sliced fresh mozzarella (optional)
2 shallots, thinly sliced
½ cup chopped smoked almonds
1 cup baby arugula

In a small saucepan set over medium heat, combine the chili sauce, honey, vinegar, oil, and sea salt and black pepper to taste. Let it come up to a simmer, then turn off the heat. Cool for a few minutes and then allow this "soak" to sit in the refrigerator for about 10 minutes.

Meanwhile, arrange the watermelon and mozzarella slices (if using) on a large platter. Slowly pour the spicy honey soak over the watermelon and cheese, taking care to fully coat the pieces. Top with the shallots, chopped almonds, and arugula, using more of anything as you see fit.

Thunder and Lightning

Legend has it that when a big storm was coming, Southern country cooks would scurry out to their gardens to gather up their ripe and ready produce. Taking care to keep precious cucumbers and tomatoes safe before the winds and rain could get to them and knock them to the ground, these dedicated home cooks would then make the very best of what was around. If you've ever tasted a perfectly ripe tomato, fresh from the vine, or a super crunchy, icy-cold cucumber, then you know as well as I do that they need little dressing up—they're wonderful just as they come. In this case, we'll add just a little bit of sweet Vidalia onion and a garlicky, herby dressing whose lemony essence serves to amplify the deliciousness of it all.

Makes 4 to 6 servings

2 to 3 heirloom tomatoes, sliced
½ pint cherry or grape tomatoes, halved or quartered
½ cup sliced sweet onion
1 cup thinly sliced cucumber
2 tablespoons lemon juice
1 teaspoon minced fresh garlic
1 tablespoon chopped fresh dill
1 tablespoon chopped chives
1 teaspoon soy sauce, tamari, or coconut aminos
1 tablespoon plain Greek yogurt
½ cup to ⅔ cup olive oil

Arrange all of the tomatoes, cucumbers, and sliced onion on a big platter or plate.

In a blender, combine the lemon juice, garlic, dill, chives, soy sauce, and Greek yogurt. With the motor running, slowly pour in the oil until the dressing comes together and is well mixed.

Drizzle the vegetables with the dressing and enjoy.

Note *These amounts are not at all exact. Use as many tomato, cucumber, and onion slices as you like.*

Three Green Tomatoes

Or charred green tomatoes with a zesty raw green tomato chowchow and loads of caramelized molasses-scented shallots. This recipe, as with several others in this book, uses one ingredient in a couple of different ways. It's a great way to showcase a specific ingredient, and in this case, we're showing off the humble green tomato. You almost always see them fried (because that's delicious). But Southern cooking embraces the green tomato in so many other, equally lovable ways.

Sweet, spicy, tangy, and texturally all over the map, this recipe may start with three green tomatoes, but it stops in a place that is complex, interesting, and downright addicting.

Makes 4 servings

3 green tomatoes
5 shallots
2 tablespoons apple cider vinegar
1 tablespoon honey
4 tablespoons olive oil, plus more as needed, divided
Salt
Freshly ground black pepper
Scant 1 teaspoon chipotle powder
1 tablespoon molasses
¼ cup chopped corn nuts, for crunch (optional)
Chopped green onions, for garnish (optional)

Dice 1 green tomato and put the diced pieces into a bowl. Mince 1 shallot and add it to the diced tomatoes, along with the vinegar, honey, and 1 tablespoon of the oil. Season with salt and pepper to taste. Let this relish sit while you prepare the rest of the dish.

Slice the 4 remaining shallots.

Slice the other 2 tomatoes into ¼-inch slices. Season them with salt and pepper to taste. Sear the tomato slices for 3 to minutes on both sides in a large, dry nonstick skillet over medium-high heat, until lightly charred and tender. Transfer to a platter.

Reduce the heat to medium and pour in the remaining 2 tablespoons of oil (this doesn't have to be exact). Add the sliced shallots and cook, stirring occasionally, for 5 minutes. Season with salt, the chipotle powder, and the molasses. Stir to mix and allow the shallots to brown and caramelize, 4 to 5 minutes more. When they're deeply golden and pseudo-crisped, scatter them across the seared green tomatoes.

Top with the green tomato relish and chopped corn nuts and chopped green onions (if using) and enjoy.

Honey-Roasted Radishes with Herby, Lemony Yogurt

I love a radish, I really do. They appear more than once in this book, my affection only growing as I continue to find ways to incorporate them into so many things. It's the uniquely peppery bite they add, coupled with an addictive crunch, that gets me every time. Here, however, we'll mellow those things out a bit and complement that peppery flavor with some honey, my preferred natural sweetener. A nod to the classic combination of radishes and sweet cream butter, I've opted to replace the latter with a puddle of punchy, citrusy yogurt, whose tangy flavor suits the radishes really well.

Makes 2 to 4 servings as an appetizer or snack

16 to 18 (about 2 bunches) red or Easter Egg radishes, washed, trimmed, and halved, plus a few extra radishes, sliced, for serving (optional)

Olive oil, for coating
2 tablespoons honey
Salt
Freshly ground black pepper
¾ cup Herby, Lemony Yogurt (page 21)

Preheat the oven to 400°F. Adjust the rack to the top position. Line a large baking sheet with parchment paper or a silicone baking mat.

Put the radishes on the prepared baking sheet and drizzle with enough oil to coat. Add the honey and season to taste with salt and pepper. Roast until softened and nicely browned, 20 to 25 minutes, stirring once halfway through.

Spoon the lemony yogurt onto a plate or platter and pile the roasted radishes on top. Arrange any raw radish slices in and around the roasted ones, if desired.

Raw and Roasted Grapes with Shaved Carrots and Blue Cheese

If you look closely, there's an old-fashioned carrot-raisin salad in here. But in my hot take, I've added a ton of flavor and interest by swapping in colorful, juicy grapes for the raisins and sprinkling on just a little blue cheese and fresh herbs. This is a favorite of mine, and it works well on just about any table, any time of year. By serving one ingredient in two simple ways—raw and roasted—on a plate, you get more bang for your buck and you really flex all the muscles of that ingredient.

Makes 4 servings

3 cups red or black grapes, divided
3 cups green grapes, divided
Maple syrup
¼ cup olive oil, plus more for drizzling, divided
Salt
Freshly ground black pepper
10 to 12 large carrots
2 tablespoons freshly minced chives

2 tablespoons chopped fresh dill
1 tablespoon Dijon mustard
2 teaspoons honey
2 teaspoons apple cider vinegar
2 tablespoons plain Greek or regular yogurt
⅔ cup crumbled blue cheese (feta or goat cheese work as well)
Arugula or watercress, for serving

Preheat the oven to 375°F. Adjust the rack to the top position.

Put about 4 cups of the grapes, 2 cups of each color, on a large baking sheet and drizzle with maple syrup to taste and enough oil to coat (a couple of teaspoons or so). Season with salt and pepper to taste. Roast for 20 to 25 minutes, or until slumped and beginning to caramelize.

Meanwhile, halve the remaining 1 cup of red grapes and remaining 1 cup of green grapes. Using a vegetable peeler, shave the carrots into long ribbon-like strands. Combine the halved raw grapes and carrots in a large bowl along with the chives and dill.

In a medium bowl, stir together the mustard, honey, vinegar, and yogurt. While stirring, slowly pour in the remaining ¼ cup of oil, or enough to get it to your preferred consistency. Season to taste with salt and pepper, and adjust as needed (more acid, more salt, etc.).

When the grapes have roasted, add them to the bowl with the carrots and raw grapes and, adding a little dressing at a time, toss gently until coated and mixed. Pile onto a serving platter and top with blue cheese and arugula or watercress.

SPOTLIGHT

You'll end up with extra, unused carrot cores after peeling. To ensure nothing is wasted, just put them in a freezer-safe bag and freeze them to use in future soups and stocks (such as Southern Summer Concentrate, page 20).

Warm Broccoli and White Bean Spoon Salad

This recipe is truly greater than the sum of its parts. Simple and unassuming— we're talking beans, broccoli, and raisins, after all—this one just might surprise you.

Driven by my unending search for new ways to serve beans (because beans are the greatest), this recipe highlights their buttery creaminess beautifully by adding some smoky, crunchy broccoli, salty anchovies (trust me on this one), and a buoying pop of sweetness from golden raisins. You can mix and match things here though— adding in some chickpeas, swapping in charred asparagus or zucchini for the broccoli, etc. It's the naturally sweet and salty combination that just really hits.

Makes 4 servings

8 cups fresh broccoli florets (approximate; I use enough to cover a standard baking sheet)
2 tablespoons olive oil, plus more for coating
Salt
Freshly ground black pepper
½ cup chopped sweet onion
5 anchovies, finely chopped
½ cup golden raisins
2 (15-ounce) cans white beans (such as butter beans, chickpeas, cannellini, or great northern), rinsed and drained
⅔ cup shaved or grated Parmesan cheese
Lemon, for serving

Preheat the oven to 425°F. Adjust the rack to the middle position.

Put the broccoli onto a large baking sheet, toss with enough oil to coat the florets all over, and season generously with salt and pepper to taste. Roast until deeply browned and the tops are charred and crispy, 20 to 25 minutes, tossing halfway through.

Meanwhile, set a large skillet over medium heat and pour in 2 tablespoons of oil. When the oil is hot, add the onion, anchovies, and raisins and cook for 6 to 8 minutes, until the onion is soft and the anchovies are brown and smell nutty.

Gently stir in the beans, followed by the charred broccoli, and let everything warm through. Sprinkle with Parmesan cheese and a little salt and pepper to taste. Finish with a squeeze of lemon and another drizzle of oil, if desired.

Copper Pennies

This is my modern spin on a vintage veggie recipe that I've always found charming. It's probably the name. Traditionally, "copper pennies" feature cooked carrots, onion, and bell peppers that swim in a mixture of tomato sauce, lots of sugar, and vegetable oil. This is a decidedly lighter spin that is not only better for you but also so much more delicious, thanks to the spicy kick from the shishitos and the sweet brightness of balsamic vinegar. These carrots are coated in a sticky-sweet glaze that is kissed with just a little bit of honey—no refined sugar need apply.

Makes 4 to 6 servings

1 tablespoon olive oil
1 pound carrots, sliced into ⅛-inch coins
Salt
Freshly ground black pepper
1 heaping cup diced onion
1 heaping cup thinly sliced shishito peppers (1 seeded and chopped poblano would also work)
1 cup canned tomato sauce
2 tablespoons honey
1 tablespoon Worcestershire sauce
1 tablespoon balsamic vinegar
Chopped fresh herbs for topping (such as cilantro, parsley, dill, and scallions)

Pour the oil into a large skillet set over medium heat. When the oil is shimmering hot, add the carrots, season with salt and black pepper to taste, and cook, stirring occasionally, for 5 minutes. Add the onion and shishitos. Cook, stirring occasionally, for 3 to 5 minutes, or until the veggies are nice and tender.

Add the tomato sauce, honey, Worcestershire sauce, and vinegar. Cook for 3 to 5 minutes, so the glaze can thicken. The carrots should be tender-crisp, with just a little bite in them left after cooking. Shower with lots of fresh green herbs before serving and enjoy either as a cold salad or warm, as a side dish.

Green Beans and Fennel With Beet Hummus and Lemony Walnuts

The South is famous for its mile-high layered vegetable salads, and I suppose this recipe is my nod to that fact. Creamy, crunchy, and as colorful as can be, this recipe looks so impressive, but (between us) it is incredibly simple to prepare. We'll take some major time-saving help from the store and use premade hummus and canned beets for the electric pink spread that gets slathered all over the platter, anchoring the veggies to follow. Feel free to make your favorite hummus recipe, if you like, and you can roast fresh beets as well. But this shortcut will lead you to the same delicious place in a fraction of the time. From one home cook to another, sometimes you've just got to keep it real.

Makes 4 to 6 servings

1 bulb fennel, trimmed and sliced into ¼-inch rings (save the feathery green tops, the fronds, for garnishing)
1 pound fresh green beans, trimmed
4 tablespoons olive oil, divided
Salt
Freshly ground black pepper
1 cup store-bought hummus
6 canned whole beets
1 cup walnut halves (salted if you can find them)
Zest of 1 lemon
⅔ cup corn nuts (optional)

Preheat the oven to 425°F. Adjust the rack to the top position.

Put the fennel rings and green beans on a large baking sheet. Drizzle with 2 tablespoons of the oil. Season with salt and pepper to taste. Roast for 22 to 25 minutes, or until tender and lightly golden brown, stirring halfway through.

Meanwhile, put the hummus and beets in a food processor and process on high until smooth and creamy. Spread the beet hummus on a large platter.

Put the walnuts in a small skillet over medium heat. Toast, stirring occasionally, until they just become fragrant, 3 to 4 minutes. Transfer to a bowl, add the remaining 2 tablespoons of oil, the lemon zest, and the corn nuts (if using). Stir to mix.

To serve, pile the roasted beans and fennel on top of the beet hummus. Sprinkle with the lemony walnuts and corn nuts. Garnish with the reserved chopped fennel fronds.

Southern Killed Lettuces

The classic Southern wilted salad, or "killed lettuces," features a warm dressing made from rendered bacon fat. It is delicious by all accounts but very rich and heavy, too. In this version, we'll still use tons of crunchy green lettuces (I like frisée, butter, little gems, and romaine), but we'll drench them with a more healthful skillet-warmed dressing. Olive oil, apple cider vinegar, smoky chipotle pepper, and chopped peanuts combine in a dressing so tasty you might find yourself using it on/in/ around more than just lettuce.

Makes 4 to 6 servings

8 cups mixed lettuces, washed and dried (such as romaine, little gems, butter, and frisée)
¾ cup sliced sweet onion (or as much as you like)
¾ cup sliced cucumber
¾ cup olive oil
¼ cup apple cider vinegar
1 chipotle pepper, minced
1 teaspoon honey or maple syrup
1 cup dry-roasted peanuts, chopped
1 teaspoon minced or grated garlic
Salt
Freshly ground black pepper

Arrange the lettuces on either a large platter or divide them among individual plates. Top with the sliced onion and cucumber.

Set a medium skillet (preferably nonstick) over medium heat and combine the oil, vinegar, minced chipotle, honey, chopped peanuts, and garlic. Whisk to mix and blend everything, and season with salt and pepper to taste. Bring to a simmer and let the dressing bubble gently for 2 to 3 minutes. Pour the hot dressing evenly over the salad and serve.

Warm, Garlicky Beans with Shaved Cheese

I don't know if citrusy, garlic-laced, olive-oil drenched beans scream "comfort" to everyone, but I would happily tuck into a big plate of this anytime the opportunity presented itself. Beans are some kind of sacred in the South, and with good reason. Wonderfully affordable, accessible, and versatile, they're also a wholesome ingredient that will last basically forever. This recipe, in an effort to keep things fast and easy for you, actually flexes the power of canned beans. We'll infuse them with some flavorful supporting things and warm them in a pan, mostly just to knock the tinny, canned vibes away. This is good alongside whatever you want, but I especially love it with Jezebel Chicken (page 177). The tasty juices all run together, and it's the very best thing.

Makes 4 servings

2 (15-ounce) cans pinto beans, drained and rinsed (or butter beans)
½ cup olive oil
2 garlic cloves, thinly sliced
Zest of 1 lemon
Zest of 1 orange
2 to 3 teaspoons apple cider vinegar or white or red wine vinegar (to taste, really)
Sea salt
Freshly ground black pepper
½ cup shaved Gouda or Parmesan cheese (or any hard, salty cheese you like)

In a large pan over medium heat, combine the beans, oil, garlic, lemon zest, orange zest, vinegar, and salt and pepper to taste.

Let everything get nice and warm, which takes 4 to 5 minutes, stirring occasionally so the garlic doesn't burn. Transfer everything to a plate or serving platter and shower with the cheese to taste.

FIRE LIGHTS

*I met the BB-Cue King once, while waiting
in line at the butcher counter. His reflection
in the glass case grinned at mine.*

*I had an eighteen-pound sack of charcoal
briquettes slung over my shoulder, and
a basket filled with grilling-adjacent
kitchenware, and other such miscellany. He
could tell I hadn't done much grilling—my
overcompensation preceded me. I reeked of it.*

*Okay then, first-timer. It don't matter what
make or model the grill is or how fancy the tools.
You just need a good fire, some woodsmoke,
and a whole lotta time. My pit is like my
church, see. It's sacred; where I make my art.*

*Of all the senses, the most useful one when
you're grilling is the common one. It'll get you
where you want to go. It's okay to mess up.*

*Carefully, he slipped his wrapped packages into
his basket. I caught eyes with the clerk behind
the counter. She mouthed the word "legend."*

*Chuckling mostly to himself now, the BB-
Cue King turned to go. "Smoke 'em if you've
got 'em!" his shirt back read. He hummed
"The Thrill Is Gone" as he walked out of
the store, making his way back to church.*

"Pulled" BBQ Spaghetti-Squash Sandwiches

This has got to be one of the most unusual sandwiches I have ever made, but man is this combination a hit in my house. Tangled strands of roasted spaghetti squash mimic the fatty pork in a classic meaty version, making for a lighter, more nutritious way to get your fix. A unique and tasty scratch BBQ sauce (My Favorite BBQ Sauce, page 25) coats things perfectly, and I like to pile on some simple slaw for a cooling crunch. The Halloumi and miso? They aren't even remotely Southern, y'all. But they're two of my all-time favorite flavor weapons, and they really help to lift the squash up, transforming this into a truly magical sandwich.

Makes 4 to 6 sandwiches

1 spaghetti squash
5 teaspoons olive oil, divided
1 (8-to 10-ounce) block Halloumi cheese, cut into ¼-inch slices (feta, smoked Gouda, and smoked cheddar are also great but should not be toasted)
Salt
Freshly ground black pepper
½ small sweet onion, chopped
1 teaspoon smoked paprika or ground chipotle powder
3 garlic cloves, minced
3 tablespoons apple cider vinegar, plus more if desired
2 tablespoons molasses
2 tablespoons white miso
1 tablespoon maple syrup
¾ cup ketchup
4 to 6 whole wheat buns, toasted
½ pound prepared coleslaw or Citrusy Poppy Seed Coleslaw (page 29)

Preheat the oven to 375°F.

Roast the squash whole, directly on your oven rack, for 30 minutes. Remove from the oven and allow to cool until it has softened considerably and is easily handled. Slice in half, width-wise, scoop out the seeds, and, using a fork, scrape out the "spaghetti strands" into a large bowl until you've emptied each half; set aside.

Pour 3 teaspoons of the oil into a large nonstick skillet set over medium-high heat. When it's hot, add the sliced Halloumi and toast for 2 to 3 minutes, or just until golden brown and crisped on 1 side. Transfer to a plate and set aside. Don't wipe out the pan (we'll use that flavor).

Put the squash strands in the same skillet and season with salt and pepper to taste. Press the squash down in the pan, allowing it to really form a crust on the bottom, and let it toast up until it's dark brown and crusty—almost burnt. Turn off the heat.

Meanwhile, in a medium saucepan set over medium heat, add the remaining 2 teaspoons of oil, the chopped onion, and the paprika. Season with salt and pepper to taste. Cook until the onion is very tender, 6 to 8 minutes, stirring occasionally.

Add the garlic, stir, and cook for another 30 seconds or so. Add the vinegar, molasses, miso, and maple syrup. Stir and cook for about 1 minute. Add the ketchup, reduce the heat to low, and simmer (partially cover with the lid to catch splatters) for another 2 minutes. Transfer the mixture to a blender and blend until smooth. Add about half of the BBQ sauce to the pan with the squash and toss to mix. Add more if you like, but I save the rest for topping and dipping.

To assemble, divide the toasted Halloumi between the bun bottoms. Pile the BBQ "pulled" squash onto the Halloumi and top with some slaw and extra sauce. Finish with the bun tops and enjoy.

Dry-Rubbed Greens with Crispy Kale Chips

Southern-style greens recipes so often call for fatty cuts of pork and their renderings as both flavor and cooking mechanisms. But I am here to tell you that there are plenty of light and healthful ways to infuse your greens with deep flavor, and this recipe is filled with them. My spice blend makes a great "rub" here, but go ahead and use whatever you like. The elephant in the room here is the anchovy paste. I know, I know, it might make you want to roll your eyes, but anchovies are an excellent source of healthy-salty-fatty goodness, and dark and leafy greens stand up to them perfectly. Trust me! This is easily my favorite way to enjoy a big skillet of greens, and the crunchy kale chips add another layer of perfection.

Makes 4 servings

5 cups raw whole kale leaves (any variety you like)
2 tablespoons olive oil, plus more for drizzling
Salt
BBQ Spice Blend (page 25) or a store-bought rub/blend
½ cup finely chopped onion
1 teaspoon anchovy paste or 3 minced anchovies
10 cups shredded dark leafy greens (kale, collard, turnip, mustard, chard, etc.)
2 teaspoons apple cider vinegar or balsamic vinegar
1 teaspoon molasses
2 garlic cloves, minced or grated
Toasted sesame seeds, for topping (optional)

Preheat the oven to 350°F. Adjust the rack to the middle position.

Put the kale leaves on a large baking sheet in a single layer. Drizzle with oil to coat, season lightly with salt and generously with the spice blend (or to taste). Toss and massage to rub the mix into the kale leaves, ensuring they are well coated. Roast for 5 to 7 minutes, or until very crispy and lightly browned.

Meanwhile, pour the remaining 2 tablespoons of oil into a large skillet set over medium heat. Add the onion and anchovy paste and cook for 3 to 4 minutes. When the mixture begins to smell more nutty than fishy, this is when to add the greens.

Once the greens are all in the pan, stir to coat and add the vinegar and molasses. Add some spice blend, as much as you see fit. Cook, stirring occasionally, for 5 minutes, until the greens are wilted and slumped down.

During the last minute of cooking, add the garlic. Serve immediately with the kale chips piled on top, and a sprinkling of sesame seeds, if you like.

Brown Sugar and Chile-Crusted Baked Chicken Wings with Buttermilk-Chive Dipping Sauce

This is my most-requested recipe at home, the single thing my family adores above all else. So there's that. But also, this is the best chicken wing recipe I've tried—just so effective and truly easy to pull off. Spiced, crispy, and incredibly juicy, these things have got a lot going for themselves, and there's no frying involved whatsoever. Taking time to crack open a mess of whole black peppercorns is absolutely worth doing, as it takes the flavor profile of these wings up and all the way over the top.

Makes 12 wings

FOR THE WINGS

1 heaping tablespoon black peppercorns

1 ½ tablespoons brown sugar (light or dark)

2 tablespoons ancho chile powder (regular chili powder also works)

3 teaspoons baking soda

1 to 2 teaspoons salt

⅓ cup neutral cooking oil (canola, vegetable, or regular olive oil)

12 bone-in, skin-on chicken wings

Shishito peppers and/or sliced pickled jalapeños (optional)

FOR THE BUTTERMILK-CHIVE DIPPING SAUCE

⅔ cup mayonnaise

⅓ cup buttermilk (or more/ less, depending on your consistency preference)

1 to 2 tablespoons chopped chives

2 teaspoons apple cider vinegar

Freshly ground black pepper

To make the wings: Place the peppercorns on a large baking sheet and, using a heavy-bottom implement such as a cast-iron skillet or a mixing bowl (this is what I use since I'm using it anyway), crush the peppercorns until they're mostly cracked. You don't have to get every single one, just most of them. Rock the skillet or bowl over the peppercorns so the edges can crack them open. Pour the cracked pepper into a large mixing bowl.

To the pepper, add the brown sugar, chile powder, baking soda, and salt. Slowly pour in the oil until you have something that resembles very wet sand. Taste it for seasoning, and add more salt if you think it needs it.

Add the wings to the bowl and toss well to fully coat on all sides (see Note). Allow the mixture to marinate the wings for 30 minutes at room temperature.

Meanwhile, preheat the oven to 350°F. Adjust the rack to the middle third of the oven.

Line a large baking sheet with parchment paper and arrange the wings in a single layer. Arrange the peppers (if using) all around the wings. Bake for 35 minutes, rotating the pan halfway through.

Broil on high for 1 to 2 minutes at the end, to get the skin nice and crispy. If things already look really good—browned and cooked—you can skip this step. Just watch out and be sure the sugar doesn't burn.

To make the buttermilk-chive dipping sauce: Combine the mayonnaise, buttermilk, chives, vinegar, and pepper to taste in a small bowl, stir to mix well, and serve with the wings.

Note *You can really flavor these as heavily as you like. If you want a thicker layer of spice paste on your wings, go for it. More is more.*

Chicken Sausage, Apple, and Red Cabbage Bake

The hot and spicy linked sausages that are often available at BBQ spots and Southern smokehouses are pretty irresistible. My whole family loves them, kids included. So this recipe is somewhat inspired by them, though I'm using a decidedly leaner chicken sausage here. As beautiful as it is healthy, this is a simply satisfying bake that, while nice all year round, is particularly good in the autumn months. Feel free to use whatever flavor of chicken sausage you like, and the same goes for the apples. I usually opt for Golden Delicious or some type of red apple, but just go with what you like. The red cabbage gently stains the sweet apples, creating an alluring, rosy-hued scene.

Makes 4 servings

24 ounces fingerling potatoes, halved
2 tablespoons olive oil, plus more for brushing and drizzling
Salt
Freshly ground black pepper
BBQ Spice Blend (page 25) or store-bought spice blend (optional)
½ large red cabbage, halved, cored, and cut into 8 wedges
1 fresh garlic bulb, halved crosswise so the cloves are exposed
4 or 5 chicken sausages (any flavor you like)
1 red onion, cut into thick slices or wedges
2 apples, seeded and roughly sliced into large wedges (no peeling necessary)
Spicy brown or whole-grain mustard, for serving

Preheat the oven to 425°F. Adjust the oven rack to the center position. Line a large baking sheet with parchment paper.

Place the potatoes on the prepared baking sheet and coat with about 2 tablespoons of the oil. Season well with salt, pepper, and a generous sprinkle of spice blend (if using). Toss to coat. Put the cabbage wedges in a roasting pan, brush with some oil, and season with salt and pepper to taste. Tuck in the garlic bulb halves and drizzle each with a little oil.

Cover the cabbage pan with aluminum foil. Roast the pan of potatoes and the pan of cabbage and garlic together in the oven for 15 minutes (this is their head start).

After 15 minutes, give the potatoes a flip. Place back in the oven to finish cooking; it takes a total of about 40 minutes. Also, uncover the cabbage and add the sausages, onion, and apples to the roasting pan. Roast, uncovered, for 20 to 25 minutes more, or until the sausages are split and cooked through.

Combine everything in either pan or on a platter and serve with lots of mustard and the soft roasted garlic (which should squeeze easily out of the bulb).

Note *To cut the spicy punch of mustard, mix in a little bit of plain yogurt, if you like. Also, if you'd like to further crisp and char the cabbage, transfer the other ingredients to a serving dish and put the cabbage back in the oven, with the broiler on low, for 5 to 6 minutes.*

Broiled Flank Steak with Plums and Chili-Garlic Oil

My initial sketch for this recipe was so much more involved than what you see here. I'd planned this intricate sauce of mustards, roasted plums, and many seasonings. Long story short, I ultimately realized that plums need nothing more than heat—an intense blast from a broiler—to soften and sweeten into custardy cups of absolute perfection. So I just threw them on the pan with the beef and let them go. Flank steak has replaced my former go-to of rib eye, as it is much leaner.

It does, however, require a marinade to help caramelize and flavor the meat from the inside out. This recipe can be easily prepared on an outdoor grill or on a stovetop grill pan, but regardless of the heat source, flank steak is best when cooked to medium-rare and sliced very thinly.

Makes 4 servings

1 (1¾- to 2-pound) flank steak
¾ cup olive oil, divided
¼ cup apple cider vinegar
3 tablespoons soy sauce
3 tablespoons coconut sugar
6 plums, halved or quartered
Salt
Freshly ground black pepper
2 tablespoons store-bought chili-garlic sauce

Put the steak in a large zip-top plastic bag (or something comparable). Add ½ cup of the oil, the vinegar, soy sauce, and coconut sugar. Seal the bag and rub to work the marinade into and all over the meat. Let it marinate at room temperature for 1 hour.

Preheat the broiler to high. Transfer the beef to a large baking sheet and scatter the plums all around it. Season everything, plums included, with salt and pepper to taste. Broil without flipping until the meat is medium-rare on the inside, and still quite pink (130°F to 140°F). It should be nice and crusty brown on top; it takes 10 to 12 minutes. Let the steak rest for at least 10 minutes before slicing thinly.

Stir the chili-garlic sauce and remaining ¼ cup of oil together in a small bowl. Serve with the sliced steak and plums as a drizzle and/or dip (I won't tell you how to eat it—just that you should).

Blackened Cauliflower Steaks with Garlicky Scallions

And by steak, I really mean "steak." The word, as it's used in this recipe, refers to the cut that we'll use. I'm talking big, thick, formidable slabs of cauliflower that really do look great on a plate and are absolutely primed (puns always intended) to soak up the garlicky, almost drinkably delicious scallion sauce. A screaming-hot oven, a piquant seasoning mix, and a generous drenching of olive oil work together to create a blackened appearance and deep flavor all over these pieces of humble cauliflower.

Makes 4 servings

2 heads cauliflower, leafy greens and thick stems removed

½ cup olive oil, plus more for coating

½ cup store-bought blackening spice blend

2 scallions, white and green parts, finely chopped

1 heaping teaspoon minced fresh garlic

1 teaspoon apple cider vinegar

2 teaspoons chopped fresh parsley

2 teaspoons chopped fresh cilantro (optional)

Salt

Freshly ground black pepper

Preheat the oven to 500°F. Adjust the oven rack to the center position.

Slice each head of cauliflower down the center, dividing them into 2 halves. From each half, cut a 1-inch "steak" by slicing down longways (not crossways). If your cauliflower heads are big enough, you might be able to cut a second steak from each half. If not, you can still roast the remaining cauliflower pieces right alongside the larger steaks.

Put the cauliflower steaks and any extra "steak bites" on a large baking sheet and coat each piece with oil, followed by a generous amount of blackening spice; ¾ to 1 teaspoon per steak. Coat any smaller pieces with blackening spice as well.

Roast until deeply browned and tender, about 25 minutes.

Meanwhile, add the chopped scallions, garlic, vinegar, parsley, and cilantro (if using) to a small bowl. Add the ½ cup of oil, ensuring that you use enough to completely cover the ingredients. Season with salt and pepper to taste, and serve alongside (and all over) the blackened cauliflower.

Honey-Caramelized Tomato Upside-Down Cornbread

People get very territorial about their cornbread in the South, a fact that I have always found completely charming. Home cooks are devoted to their recipes and food traditions in a way that serves to sustain them, carrying them across generations. There is so much heart on the table, always. Cooks hold on tight to them, their family recipes, and it's really the most beautiful thing. This recipe happens to be a favorite version of cornbread in my house. The jammy, juicy-sweet tomatoes suspended on top really do steal this show, and the olive oil makes it pretty special. Feel free to sub a different cooking oil, though, as olive oil ain't cheap. I highly recommend serving this in thick slices, slathered with lots of Salty Butter–Whipped Honey (page 28).

Makes 6 to 8 servings

Natural nonstick cooking spray
12 ounces cherry or
   grape tomatoes
6 tablespoons honey, divided
1½ teaspoons salt, plus
   more as needed
1 cup yellow cornmeal

1 cup cake flour
1½ teaspoons baking powder
1 teaspoon baking soda
⅔ cup olive oil or canola
   or vegetable oil
2 large eggs, beaten
1¼ cups buttermilk

Preheat the oven to 350°F. Adjust the rack to the middle position. Spray an 8- or 9-inch round cake pan with cooking spray and line with parchment paper, allowing some overhang for easy removal (think of them as handles).

Put the tomatoes, 3 tablespoons of the honey, and a good pinch of salt in a nonstick skillet set over medium heat and cook, stirring occasionally, until the tomatoes just burst and are tender, about 5 minutes. Transfer to the cake pan, juices included, and spread in an even layer.

In a mixing bowl, whisk together the cornmeal, remaining 1½ teaspoons salt, cake flour, baking powder, and baking soda.

In the bowl of a stand mixer or in a mixing bowl with a handheld mixer, combine the oil, the remaining 3 tablespoons of honey, and the eggs. Add half of the dry mixture and mix until combined. Add half of the buttermilk and mix until just combined. Repeat with the remaining halves of each and gently pour the batter into the prepared pan over the tomatoes (it shouldn't be more than three-fourths full).

Bake until lightly golden and set, 35 to 45 minutes (use a knife or toothpick to test the doneness—it should come out clean). Cool in the pan for at least 15 minutes before inverting the cornbread onto a serving plate, tomatoes facing up now.

Peel off the parchment paper before serving (I'm sure you knew this already, but still). This will keep covered at room temperature for about 2 days and in the fridge for 3 or 4 days. If wrapped well, it will also freeze for up to 2 months.

Lace Hoecakes

This was the very first recipe I ever cooked by myself, and, as such, it hovers pretty close to my heart. These lacy little cakes are the thinner, wafter-like alternative to cornbread, and they're so easy to make. With only a few ingredients, this is such a great back-pocket recipe to have around in a pinch. The edges of these classic Southern-style griddle cakes frizzle and bubble out into a lacy, doily-like web of sorts, giving them their name. Rather than frying these up in the traditional bacon grease, I typically reach for healthier alternatives like ghee or olive oil. The deliciousness doesn't depend on bacon fat here but rather on the crisp texture and well-seasoned batter. Piled up on a platter, these lacy wafers are perfect on any table from breakfast to dinner, but I especially love them as part of a BBQ spread.

Makes about 24 hoecakes

2 cups sifted yellow cornmeal
2 ½ cups vegetable stock or water
1 teaspoon salt
Ghee, canola oil, or grapeseed oil, for cooking

Whisk together the cornmeal, stock, and salt.

Spoon a little bit of ghee into a large nonstick skillet (or flat hoe skillet, if you have one) set over medium heat. When it's shimmering hot, and working in batches, pour a scant ¼ cup of batter into the skillet.

When the edges are slightly brown, after 3 to 4 minutes, use a large spatula to carefully flip the hoecake, allowing the other side to cook for an additional 1 minute or so, until golden brown. The middles will be more cake-like, and the edges will be lacy.

Be sure to stir the batter (it will settle and separate on you) and add a little more oil to the skillet in between hoecakes.

Baked-Bean Mac and Cheese

Two classic BBQ sides combine here in a cozy, flavor-blasted dish that makes itself at home in a hurry. The lightening is in the ratio of it all, if you're wondering, as this recipe really shows off my go-to pasta trick. I cook only half of the typical amount and then supplement with something wholesome. In this case? Creamy, hearty pinto beans fit the bill. We'll also see the second act of My Favorite BBQ sauce (page 25) in this recipe—the same one we used in the "Pulled" Spaghetti-Squash BBQ Sandwiches (page 144). Here, it's fortified with some creamy garlic and herb cheese spread, healthy cottage cheese, and a reasonable amount of cheddar cheese. No sugar, cream, or butter here! With half the amount of pasta and a fraction of the typical amount of cheese, this truly indulgent-tasting recipe is actually deceptively light.

Makes 4 servings

Salt
½ pound elbow macaroni
2 teaspoons olive oil
⅓ cup diced onion
2 large garlic cloves, minced
¼ cup apple cider vinegar
1 tablespoon molasses
2 tablespoons white miso
2 tablespoons maple syrup
1 cup plus 2 tablespoons ketchup
1 (15-ounce) can pinto beans, rinsed and drained
4 ounces garlic and herb cheese spread (such as Boursin or Alouette)
1 cup cottage cheese
¾ cup milk or buttermilk
1 heaping cup freshly shredded sharp cheddar cheese
Freshly ground black pepper
Fresh basil, for garnish (optional)

Preheat the oven to 375°F. Adjust the rack to the middle position.

In a large pot of generously salted water, prepare the pasta according to the package directions. Drain and return to the pot; set aside.

Meanwhile, pour the oil into a saucepan set over medium heat. Add the onion and sauté until lightly golden. Add the garlic and cook for 30 seconds. Add the vinegar, molasses, miso, and maple syrup. Cook for 1 minute, stirring, then add the ketchup and let the mixture simmer, covered, for 5 minutes.

Add the beans, cheese spread, and cottage cheese to the sauce mixture and gently fold to mix. Pour this in the pasta pot, then add the milk and three-fourths of the cheddar. Season with salt and pepper to taste, and stir to combine. Adjust the flavors to your liking and transfer the mixture to a large skillet. Top with the remaining cheese and bake until bubbly and just beginning to brown, about 25 minutes. If desired, garnish with fresh basil.

NIGHT LIGHTS

*A quick bite standing at the kitchen counter,
or an elaborate, multicourse affair.
Table for one, table for twenty.
Fine china or paper plates.*

*A place for nourishment and
full-bellied laughs
For brand new flavors
and recipes you know by heart.*

They call it "supper" in the South.

*A dash of this, pinch of that.
Bits of the bread we break.
Something made from nothing,
with your own two hands,
wrapped up in such amazing grace.*

*From simple to sacred, taking your seat at the
dinner table can be no big thing,
or it can be everything.*

*A lifetime of memories, strung
together like party lights.*

All those big-little moments.

The glowing, bright spots after our long days.

Frico Chicken in a Garlicky Buttermilk Bath

I've taken the things I love most about classic Southern fried chicken and remixed them into something that is just as satisfying, but much lighter—a true win-win. A frico (which means "fried" in Italian) is simply a baked cheese crisp, and here we'll use them to almost mimic the salty crunch of fried chicken skin. Rather than rich bone-in, skin-on cuts, we'll use leaner boneless and skinless thighs— my favorite protein of them all. The garlicky buttermilk-fortified bath in which they cook mimics my go-to fried chicken brine, helping the chicken stay tender and juicy. It also happens to be an easy, one-pan, 30-minute meal. So there's that.

Makes 4 to 6 servings

1 ½ cups grated
    Parmesan cheese
4 teaspoons olive oil, divided
6 boneless, skinless
    chicken thighs
Salt
Freshly ground black pepper
1 heaping cup diced
    sweet onion
10 ounces fresh baby spinach
3 garlic cloves, minced
    or grated
½ cup dry white wine
    (optional)
1 (14.5-ounce) can crushed
    or diced tomatoes
½ cup buttermilk

Preheat the oven to 350°F. Adjust the oven rack to the middle position. Line a large baking sheet with parchment paper or a silicone baking mat.

Equally space the Parmesan into 6 (¼-cup) mounds on the baking sheet. Use your measuring cup to gently press down on the mounds and work them into round, circular disks (they don't have to be perfect). Bake until flattened and just beginning to brown lightly around the edges, 3 to 4 minutes. Remove and set aside. They will firm up as they cool.

Pour 2 teaspoons of the oil into a large pan over medium heat. Season the chicken with salt and pepper to taste. When the oil is hot, add the chicken and brown really well on the first side; this takes 5 to 6 minutes. Flip and cook for another 1 to 2 minutes (they will finish in the sauce). Transfer to a plate and set aside.

Pour the remaining 2 teaspoons of oil into the pan. When it's hot, add the onion and spinach and sauté for 3 to 5 minutes, until the spinach is fully wilted and the onion is soft. During the last minute, add the garlic.

Stir in the wine (if using) and cook for about 1 minute to reduce it. Add the tomatoes and buttermilk and slide the chicken back into the pan. Simmer for about 10 minutes to reduce the sauce and to finish the chicken.

Lay the Parmesan fricos over the chicken just before serving. They will melt and sort of adhere to the chicken, mimicking salty chicken skin in the best way.

Creamy Chicken Meatball Country Captain

The origins of this dish are not at all Southern, a truth that can be applied to so many beloved "Southern" dishes (see also: pimiento cheese).

This gorgeous concoction actually has roots in India, but thanks to a handful of Southern women home cooks, the interest and attention given to this particular recipe swelled throughout the South after the turn of the twentieth century. Country captain is a robust and flavorful dish involving panfried chicken that is served on top of white rice, often garnished with currants or raisins, toasted nuts, and a gravy made from tomatoes and warming spices.

In this leaner, faster take, we're going to bake some chicken meatballs and simmer them in a slightly spicy curry-laced sauce that is fit to burst with flavorful characters.

Makes 4 servings

1 pound ground chicken (turkey works, too)
4 garlic cloves, minced or grated, divided
1 (2-inch) piece fresh ginger, peeled and grated, divided
1 cup diced onion, divided
2 tablespoons grated Parmesan cheese
⅔ cup panko breadcrumbs
Salt
Freshly ground black pepper
1 tablespoon olive oil
½ jalapeño, seeded and minced (optional)

2 celery stalks, chopped
1½ teaspoons curry powder
1½ teaspoons garam masala
1 (15-ounce) can crushed tomatoes
1 (15-ounce) can coconut milk
⅔ cup golden or regular raisins
Hot cooked white, brown, or wild rice, for serving
⅔ cup chopped smoked almonds, for serving
Chopped scallion greens, for serving

Preheat the oven to 425°F. Adjust the rack to the middle position. Line a large baking sheet with parchment paper.

In a large mixing bowl, combine the chicken, half of the minced garlic, half of the minced ginger, half of the onion, the Parmesan, and the panko. Season with salt and pepper to taste. Gently mix with your hands (the best tools) until evenly combined. Add more panko if it seems too wet.

Form into 12 meatballs and evenly space them on the baking sheet. Bake for 18 minutes. They'll finish cooking in the sauce.

Meanwhile, pour the oil into a large skillet set over medium heat. Add the remaining half of the onion, ginger, and garlic, and the jalapeño (if using), celery, curry powder, and garam masala to the skillet and sauté for 6 to 8 minutes.

Season with salt and pepper, then add the tomatoes and coconut milk and stir to combine. Transfer the sauce to a blender and blend until smooth. Pour back into the skillet, then add the raisins and meatballs.

Simmer for 6 to 8 minutes, so the meatballs can finish cooking. Serve over the cooked rice, and top with smoked almonds and chopped scallions.

Baking Sheet Catfish with Okra, Corn, and Tomatoes

From the Gulf Coast to the Southern Appalachians and everywhere in between, this clean, simple, fuss-free meal is one you'll find all up and down the South. Catfish being plentiful in many Southern rivers and lakes, there is no shortage of recipes supporting this fact. I grew up eating fried catfish dinners, and delicious though that may be, a simple roast is a far more healthful way to enjoy this fish. Roasting a protein on a baking rack over top of a medley of vegetables is an effective way to make the most of a baking-sheet meal. By elevating the fillets over the vegetables, you allow the heat to circulate more freely, giving both fish and veggies a better crispness and texture.

Makes 4 servings

Natural nonstick cooking spray
Kernels from 4 ears fresh corn or 10-ounces frozen corn kernels, thawed
1 pint cherry or grape tomatoes
15 ounces fresh or frozen okra, trimmed and cut into bite-size pieces (thawed if frozen)
2 teaspoons olive oil
Salt
Freshly ground black pepper
1 pound filleted fresh catfish
1 to 2 tablespoons Creole seasoning

Preheat the oven to 350°F. Adjust the rack to the middle position. Spray a baking rack with cooking spray (or coat with olive oil).

Arrange the corn, tomatoes, and okra on a large baking sheet and drizzle with the oil. Season lightly with salt and pepper. Roast for 10 minutes.

Meanwhile, pat the fish dry with paper towels. Season both sides of the fish lightly with the Creole seasoning. After the veggies have roasted for 10 minutes, take the pan out of the oven, set the baking rack over the vegetables, and gently lay the fish on the rack. Return the pan to the oven and roast for 15 to 17 minutes, or until the fish is just cooked.

Green Chili Pork with Grits Dumplings

Some like it hot, and I happen to be a member of that group. If you, too, enjoy things a little on the spicy side, then this one's for you. For this recipe, I took some favorite elements of a few classic homey dishes and married them in a single bowl. Grits make fantastic, pillowy dumplings that offer great texture to soups and stews (and lack all of the butter of classic Southern-style dumplings), and a white chicken chili recipe is made all the better by using extra-special and super-flavorful pork tenderloin. You could fire-roast some tomatillos and other aromatics and use them in place of the salsa, sure, but honestly? A good-quality, store-bought salsa verde makes this recipe fast, easy, and approachable any night of the week.

Makes 4 servings

¾ cup quick-cooking grits
¼ cup white whole wheat flour or all-purpose flour
1 tablespoon minced onion
1 teaspoon salt
½ cup buttermilk or milk
3 tablespoons olive oil, divided, plus more as needed
1½ pounds pork tenderloin, sliced into thin medallions
Salt
Freshly ground black pepper
1 small sweet onion, diced
2 large carrots, thinly sliced (no need to peel)
2 celery stalks, thinly sliced, leafy tops reserved for garnish (optional)
1 teaspoon chicken stock concentrate
2 garlic cloves, minced
2 (4-ounce) cans diced green chiles
1 (16-ounce) jar mild store-bought salsa verde
32 ounces chicken stock
Natural nonstick cooking spray

In a large mixing bowl, whisk together the grits, flour, onion, and salt.

Warm the buttermilk and 2 tablespoons of the oil in a small saucepan over medium heat. As soon as it starts to simmer, pour into the bowl with the dry ingredients (it will split and look curdled—this is fine). Stir to blend, creating the dumpling batter. Let it rest while you make the chili.

Pour the remaining 1 tablespoon of oil into a large Dutch oven or deep pot set over medium-high heat. Working in batches, if necessary, lightly season the pork with salt and pepper and brown in the hot oil, stirring once or twice, for 4 to 5 minutes per batch. Transfer to a plate and set aside.

Reduce the heat to medium and add a little more oil, if necessary. Add the onion, carrots, and celery and cook, stirring occasionally, until tender, 5 to 6 minutes. Add the stock concentrate, garlic, and chiles and cook for another minute. Add the pork with its juices back into the pot, along with the salsa verde and chicken stock. (Taste your salsa first to make sure the spice is to your liking; if it's too spicy, use less.) Stir to mix and allow the chili to simmer, uncovered, for about 10 minutes to finish cooking the pork.

Place a steamer basket (or a colander) in a large, lidded pot set over medium heat. Pour in enough water to reach just below the bottom (it should never touch the dumplings). Spray the basket or colander with cooking spray.

Working in batches as needed, use your hands to form the dumpling mixture into 1-inch balls (although really, you can make them any size you want) and gently lay them in the basket or colander, keeping a little space between each if possible. Put the lid on and allow the dumplings to steam for 5 minutes, or until firm and cooked (they'll be dense and hearty, ready to soak up the brothy chili).

To serve, divide the dumplings among soup bowls and ladle the pork chili over top. Garnish with the reserved celery greens, if desired.

Note *For a very fast version of this, you can skip the dumplings step and just serve the chili over bowls of creamy quick-cooked grits instead.*

Chicken Fricassee

Here she is, the single recipe that I have made more than any other. It's true—I've been making versions of this Cajun-style fricassee dish for nearly fifteen years and chances are, if you know me personally, I've made it for you. I am fully in love with the deep, nearly addictive flavors in the sauce, and I think this is just about the perfect recipe to make for company. It's best a day after it's made, you see. Here, I've significantly lightened up the sauce, as well as the protein components, producing a less-greasy pan of food that is still just as delicious. It can't help being a showstopper, every single time.

Makes 4 servings

4 teaspoons olive oil, plus more as needed
12 ounces smoked turkey sausage, cut into thin pieces
6 boneless, skinless chicken thighs
1½ cups diced sweet onions
2 celery stalks, diced
1 green bell pepper, diced
12-ounces sliced white or cremini mushrooms
2 large carrots, sliced into thin rounds
Salt
Freshly ground black pepper
3 garlic cloves, minced
¼ cup white whole wheat flour
⅔ cup dry white wine or a light-bodied beer
2 cups chicken stock
⅓ to ½ cup plain Greek yogurt or buttermilk
Cooked brown rice, cauliflower rice, or grits, for serving

Place a large, deep skillet over medium-high heat and pour in about 2 teaspoons of the olive oil. Cook the sausage pieces, stirring occasionally, until deeply browned and crisped all over, 3 to 4 minutes. Transfer to a bowl or plate and set aside.

In the same pan over the same heat, add the remaining 2 teaspoons of oil and, working in batches, brown the chicken thighs on both sides, 2 to 3 minutes per side. Transfer the browned chicken to a plate and set aside.

Reduce the heat to medium, then add the onions, celery, bell pepper, mushrooms, and carrots to the pan. Season lightly with salt and pepper and sauté the veggies, stirring occasionally, until nice and tender, 5 to 6 minutes. Add the garlic and the flour. Cook, stirring constantly, for about 1 minute.

Deglaze the pan with the wine, stirring to get up any browned bits. After 30 seconds, add the stock. Stir well to break up any clumps of flour and to smooth out the sauce.

Slide the chicken back into the pan, along with its juices, followed by the sausage pieces. Simmer over low heat for about 25 minutes to finish the chicken and to develop all of the flavors. Turn off the heat and stir in the yogurt. Serve warm with brown rice, cauliflower rice, or grits to sop up the sauce.

Balsamic Pear and Shallot Smothered Pork Chops

Classic for a reason, the combination of salty, succulent (I said it) pork chops and sweet, juicy fruit panders right to my sweet-and-savory-loving heart.

You can make this with any manner of sliced fruit, really. Let the seasons be your guide here. The most basic brine that we'll implement serves to ensure that the pork stays juicy, seasoned, and completely irresistible. Something I do whenever I cook pork chops, it's an easy extra step that always proves its worth. The two tablespoons of butter (yes, butter!) go a long way here, enriching and glossing out the sauce in a manner that is most necessary.

Makes 4 servings

1 quart plus ⅓ cup warm water, divided
¼ cup kosher salt, plus more for seasoning
4 thick-cut, bone-in pork chops
Freshly ground black pepper
1 tablespoon olive oil
3 shallots, thinly sliced
2 pears, cored and thinly sliced, no need to peel (I use Bartlett)
⅓ cup maple syrup
⅓ cup balsamic vinegar
1 tablespoon chicken stock concentrate
2 tablespoons butter or ghee
4 ounces crumbled goat cheese, for topping
Fresh herbs, roughly chopped, for topping (such as parsley, basil, chives and/or scallions)

To brine your chops, fill a large bowl or dish with 1 quart of the warm water and ¼ cup of the kosher salt. Stir until the salt is absorbed, then add the pork. Let the chops sit in the brine for 15 minutes. Afterward, rinse them under water to remove any excess salt. Pat dry.

Sprinkle the chops with lots of pepper and a little more salt. Pour the oil into a large skillet set over medium-high heat and, when it's shimmering hot, add the chops. Sear the pork on both sides until nice and brown, 3 to 4 minutes per side.

Preheat the broiler to high and adjust the oven rack to the middle position.

When the pork is done searing, scatter the sliced shallots and pears in the skillet, all around and over the meat. In a small bowl, mix together the maple syrup, vinegar, stock concentrate, and the remaining ⅓ cup of water. Add that mixture to the skillet—just pour it over everything. Top with bits of the butter and place under the broiler. Broil until the pork is sizzling and crisped and the fruit is tender, 4 to 5 minutes.

Serve right away topped with the crumbled goat cheese and a sprinkling of fresh herbs.

Brunswick Stew No. 3

Brunswick stew is the kind of recipe that epitomizes the practical, resourceful type of Southern cooking that I love most. Pots of this tomatoey, veggie-packed stew traditionally include additional components that vary depending on what the cook has on hand or needs to use up. I have an old copy of Southern Living's Southern Country Cookbook, *which features two versions of Brunswick stew. One contains hen and stew meat; the other, rabbit and squirrel. My version here is meatless— just packed with a bunch of colorful vegetables. The best part? We'll pull the potatoes out of the stew, roast them, and pile them on top like salty, crispy potato croutons.*

Makes 4 servings

1 teaspoon baking soda
Salt
6 cups (1-inch diced) gold potatoes
¼ cup olive oil, plus more as needed
Freshly ground black pepper
1 sweet onion, diced
2 celery stalks, diced
3 large carrots, thinly sliced (no need to peel)
2 garlic cloves, minced or grated
2 teaspoons vegetable or chicken stock concentrate
10-ounces fresh or frozen corn (if frozen, no need to thaw)

6 ounces light-bodied beer (Cook gets the rest! Or, just sub more stock)
1 (15-ounce) can crushed or diced tomatoes
1 (15-ounce) can lima beans, drained and rinsed
1 cup My Favorite BBQ Sauce (page 25) or a store-bought variety
3 cups vegetable or chicken stock
Citrusy Poppy Seed Coleslaw (page 29) or coleslaw of choice, for serving

Preheat the oven to 425°F. Line a large baking sheet with parchment paper.

Fill a large pot two-thirds full with water and add the baking soda. Salt the water like the sea and bring to a boil. Carefully add the potatoes and cook until completely fork-tender. Drain and return to the pot. Put the lid on and shake and agitate the potatoes to bust them up a bit, releasing their creamy insides. Add ¼ cup of the olive oil, a couple teaspoons of salt, and lots of pepper. Toss gently to coat.

Spread the potatoes out on the baking sheet in an even layer. Roast for 40 to 45 minutes, or until super crispy and golden brown.

Meanwhile, pour a couple teaspoons of the oil into a large Dutch oven set over medium heat. When the oil is hot, add the onion, celery, and carrots. Season lightly with salt and pepper. Cook until the veggies are tender, 6 to 8 minutes, and add more

oil as needed to keep things moving. Add the garlic, stock concentrate, and corn and cook for 1 minute.

Add the beer and cook for 2 to 3 minutes. Add the tomatoes, lima beans, BBQ sauce, and stock. Reduce the heat to low and stew the mixture, covered, for 30 minutes.

Transfer 2 cups of the stew to a blender and blend until smooth. Return to the pot and mix to combine. Serve in bowls topped with the roasted potatoes and coleslaw.

Spinach and Artichoke Pot Pie with Turkey Sausage

We're ditching the butter-filled pastry for light and airy phyllo dough in this very Mediterranean spin on a cozy classic. This can easily be made into a meatless meal by avoiding the turkey sausage and sticking with vegetable stock. If you do opt to go the meatless route, I'd recommend adding in 12 ounces of sliced mushrooms when you're sautéing the vegetables in the second step. This dish is filled with good-for-you things and has so much flavor, you won't miss the fat one bit.

Makes 6 servings

2 teaspoons olive oil, plus more for brushing

13 ounces smoked turkey sausage, cut into bite-size pieces

2 teaspoons Greek seasoning or oregano

1 cup diced onion

2 celery stalks, chopped

2 large carrots, cut into ¼- to ½-inch pieces

1 large russet potato, diced

Salt

Freshly ground black pepper

1 (10-ounce) package frozen spinach, thawed and squeezed of any excess water

1 (12- to 15-ounce) can or jar artichoke hearts, drained (marinated or not)

3 garlic cloves, minced or grated

2 tablespoons chopped fresh dill

3 to 4 cups chicken or vegetable stock (depends on exact pan size you use)

6 ounces crumbled feta cheese

2 teaspoons cornstarch

½ package phyllo dough (about 8 ounces), thawed

Pour the 2 teaspoons of oil into a large ovenproof pan set over medium heat. When it is shimmering hot, brown the sausage, seasoning it with the Greek seasoning. It takes about 5 minutes. Transfer to a plate and set aside.

Add a little more oil to the pan if needed. Add the onion, celery, carrots, and potato. Season with salt and pepper to taste. Cook for 6 to 8 minutes, stirring occasionally, until the veggies are tender. Add the spinach, artichokes, garlic, dill, and enough stock to just cover the contents of the pan. Add the feta and stir to combine.

In a small bowl or ramekin, combine the cornstarch with 1 to 2 tablespoons of the hot broth from the pan, stirring until smooth. Pour this slurry back into the pan and stir to combine. Bring to a light boil and then reduce to a simmer while you preheat the oven and prepare the crust.

Preheat the oven to 375°F. Adjust the rack to the middle position.

Tear and pull apart pieces of phyllo dough, brush them with oil, and then shingle them all over the top of the pan allowing them to overhang (I enjoy the drama of this). This isn't a perfect or precise thing! You might very well not use as much as I've specified. This is fine. You just want it all covered, and you want the phyllo to be oiled, as this will help with browning.

Bake the pot pie for 28 to 30 minutes, or until bubbly and nicely browned on top. If parts of the crust are darkening faster than others, lay a large piece of aluminum foil over top to slow the browning down.

Let the pot pie rest for about 10 minutes before serving.

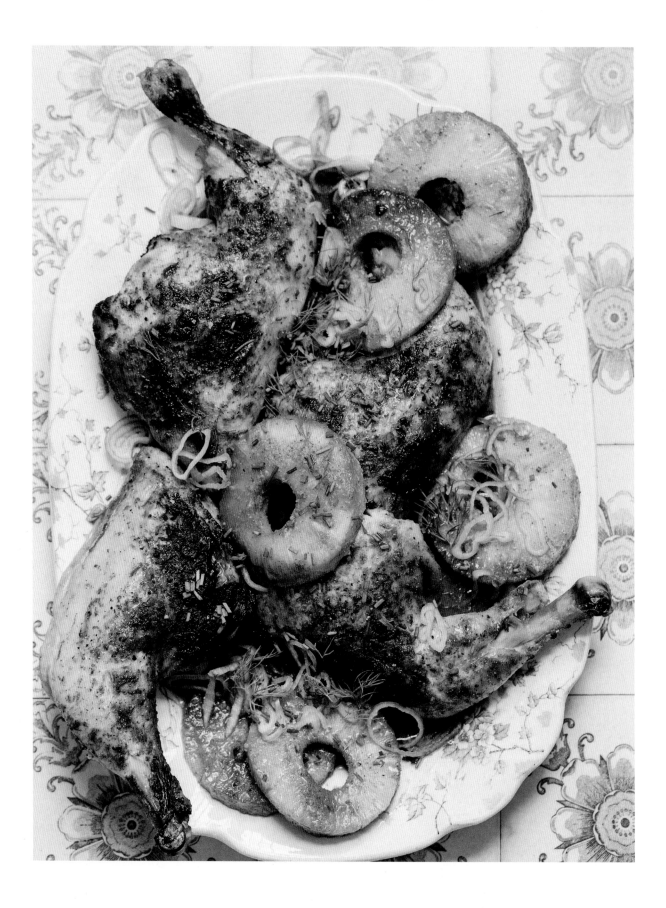

Jezebel Chicken

Have you noticed that there are a lot of chicken recipes in this book? There are, I know. It is my family's favorite, and my two kids love nothing more than juicy roasted or fried chicken. Seeing as how fried chicken is rather laborious to make and not the lightest option, I really lean into the roasting of it. Managing to be both humble and unbelievably luxurious-seeming all at once, this one takes a classic fruity-sweet Southern Jezebel sauce and uses it as a twist on what is otherwise a very basic roasted chicken recipe. The difference-maker here, though, is the salt. We'll season things the whole way through, and even so, I still like to serve roasted chicken with flaky sea salt on the side. Like a potato, a simple roasted chicken goes from unnoticeable to extraordinary once the right amount of salt is welcomed into the scene.

Makes 4 servings

4 bone-in, skin-on chicken leg quarters (this works with any cut, I just like the legs here)
1 pineapple, cored and sliced into ½-inch rings or spears
¼ cup store-bought hot honey (or regular honey)
¼ cup spicy brown mustard
¼ cup soy sauce
1 tablespoon paprika
½ teaspoon garlic powder
1 tablespoon apple cider vinegar
Salt
Freshly ground black pepper
¾ cup chopped fresh herbs, for serving (such as chives, parsley, and dill)
1 shallot, thinly sliced
Flaky sea salt, for sprinkling on top (optional)

Put the pineapple slices in a single layer in a large baking dish or sheet pan. Lay the chicken legs on top. Mix together the honey, mustard, soy sauce, paprika, garlic powder, and vinegar in a bowl and pour all over the chicken and pineapple. Rub to coat evenly and put the dish in the fridge to marinate (covered or not), for at least 1 hour and up to 4 hours.

Preheat the oven to 425°F. Adjust the rack to the middle position.

Season the chicken and pineapple with salt and lots of pepper. Cover the baking dish with aluminum foil and roast for 35 minutes. Remove the foil and roast for 20 to 25 minutes or until the chicken is cooked through and deeply browned (it will likely appear burnt in places thanks to the sugars, but worry not! It's all good).

Serve the chicken and pineapple with the drippings, a shower of chopped herbs and sliced shallot, and some sea salt if you like.

HOLIDAY LIGHTS

*The best Thanksgiving meal I've ever eaten
was on the Fourth of July.*

*I like my cranberries from a can.
I prefer to cook a chicken on Turkey Day.*

*I almost always burn the rolls, and
I break at least two ornaments per year.
My Christmas tree is a fake and a phony.*

*I care about college football rivalries
not at all.*

*Unavoidable.
Unstoppable.
Perfectly imperfect.*

*It's the weird traditions and delicious disasters
that make the holiday season
so great, if you ask me.*

They're great because they're all ours.

*So hang the lights and trim the tree
But please don't miss the forest for it.
Break glass. Break rules.
Color outside every line, if you want to.*

*Make all of your beautiful messes.
Embrace your calamities.
Season your holidays to taste.*

Pomegranate and Mandarin Relish

Charleston's warm, subtropical climate provides a happy growing place for all sorts of citrusy goodness, mandarins and lemons being my family's favorites. This recipe works just as well with canned mandarins and will come together even faster for you that way. The vibrant flavors in this colorful condiment will lighten and brighten any protein with which you choose to pair it (I love it on roasted pork or atop grilled beef). Or keep things even lighter and serve it in a bowl with whole wheat crackers or baked tortilla chips as dippers. Options abound here, and no matter how you choose to serve this, your holiday tables will be all the merrier for it.

Makes about 1½ cups

3 fresh mandarins, peeled
⅔ cup pomegranate seeds
⅓ cup chopped fresh cilantro
⅓ cup minced red onion
½ jalapeño, seeded and finely chopped, or poblano for milder heat
Juice of ½ lime
Salt
Freshly ground black pepper

Separate the mandarins into segments, just pulling them apart where they naturally separate. Cut these into smaller, bite-size pieces (I typically quarter them).

In a bowl, combine the pomegranate seeds, mandarin pieces, cilantro, onion, jalapeño, lime juice, salt, and pepper, stir to mix well, and enjoy over meats, fish, or as a beautiful dip on any table. This does taste better the longer it sits and will keep covered in the refrigerator for up to 2 weeks.

SPOTLIGHT

To remove the seeds from a pomegranate, simply slice it in half and then hold it over a bowl of water. Using a wooden spoon or something comparable, give the fruit several solid whacks to dislodge the little ruby jewels. They should fall into the bowl with relative ease.

Creamy Roasted Garlic Mashed Potatoes

Making mashed potatoes without any butter, heavy cream, cream cheese, or sour cream almost seems like a Southern sin, I know. But these potatoes are here to prove that those heavy-hitters are not necessary to create ultra-creamy, flavorful mashed potatoes. Instead, we'll build a simple yet tasty roasted garlic cream made from the healthy trifecta of yogurt, cottage cheese, and buttermilk. I wield these three ingredients so many times throughout this book, and they always hold their own beautifully. Butter, beware.

Makes 4 to 6 servings

5 large Yukon Gold potatoes, peeled or not
32 ounces chicken or vegetable stock
1 teaspoon salt, plus more
Freshly ground black pepper

1 garlic bulb, cloves separated and peeled
⅓ cup plain Greek yogurt
⅓ cup cottage cheese
⅓ cup buttermilk
Olive oil, for drizzling
Chopped chives, for garnishing

Preheat the oven to 350°F.

Cut the potatoes into 1-inch pieces, and put them in a large pot. Add the chicken stock and enough salt to make it taste salty like the sea (as with pasta water). If the potatoes aren't fully submerged in the stock, add enough water to cover by about 2 inches. Bring to a boil and cook until very fork-tender, 25 to 30 minutes. Reserve 1 cup of the salty, starchy cooking liquid, then drain. Transfer the potatoes to a large mixing bowl and set aside.

Wrap the garlic up in a piece of aluminum foil, creating a little package. Put the foil packet directly on the oven rack and roast until the cloves are very tender, 20 to 25 minutes.

Meanwhile, in a blender, combine the yogurt, cottage cheese, and buttermilk. Season with the 1 teaspoon of salt and lots of pepper. Add the roasted garlic and blend until very smooth. Pour this roasted garlic cream over the cooked potatoes and, using a handheld mixer, whip the potatoes until smooth and creamy.

Transfer to a baking or serving dish, drizzle with a little oil, and garnish with some chopped chives to finish.

See page 180 for photo.

Roasted Brussels Sprouts with Vanilla-Cayenne Glaze

"Fuzzy" is the word I'd use to describe the heat level in these sprouts. They aren't knock-your-socks-off spicy, but the presence of chile is definitely felt. Vanilla and maple combine to make the most glorious, sticky-sweet glaze, underscoring my firm belief that the inherent funk of this vegetable is best supported by something sweet. But, not to be outdone, lemon and balsamic vinegar are also nominated for best supporting actors. Because as is so often the case, acids just make everything else perform like the very best versions of themselves.

Makes 4 servings

1 ½ pounds Brussels sprouts, trimmed and halved
¼ cup olive oil, plus more as needed
¾ teaspoon salt, plus more
Freshly ground black pepper
⅓ cup maple syrup
2 teaspoons vanilla extract
1 tablespoon balsamic vinegar
¼ teaspoon cayenne pepper
Zest of 2 lemons
Finely chopped nuts (such as walnuts, peanuts, pistachios, or pecans), for topping (optional)
Flaky sea salt, for finishing (optional)

Preheat the oven to 450°F. Adjust the rack to the middle position. Line a large baking sheet with parchment paper.

Put the Brussels sprouts on the prepared baking sheet, drizzle with the oil, and season with the salt and black pepper to taste. Toss to coat and arrange them all cut-sides down. Roast until browned, crispy, and golden, 20 to 25 minutes.

Meanwhile, pour the maple syrup into a small saucepan set over medium heat. Let it bubble and simmer until it has thickened a bit, 3 to 4 minutes. Remove from the heat and add the vanilla, vinegar, and cayenne. Season lightly with salt.

Transfer the roasted sprouts to a serving platter and pour the glaze all over top, letting it just spill everywhere. Sprinkle with the lemon zest (it's meant to be a lot) and chopped nuts (if using), and season with a little extra flaky salt, if desired.

See page 180 for photo.

Quick Chicken and Apple Stuffing Skillet

This is a one-pan recipe that packs in all of the goodness you'd expect and crave from a cozy holiday meal, but it comes together in under an hour. I'm all for a table filled with rich, over-the-top, long-cooked fare, for sure. But I have found that this lighter, faster option is just as delicious and it hits all of the same notes. Turkey has never really been my thing, and when it comes to poultry, I'm going to go for juicy, flavorful, foolproof chicken thighs every time. Sensible swaps and leaner substitutions make this far healthier than a typical holiday meal, and while you might still need a nap afterward, you certainly won't feel the need to run a mini-marathon to make up for everything. There's a lot to be said for that.

Makes 4 servings

3 teaspoons olive oil, divided, plus more as needed
¾ pound ground turkey sausage
4 bone-in, skin-on chicken thighs
Salt
Freshly ground black pepper
2 teaspoons poultry seasoning
1 cup diced onion
1 green bell pepper, diced
12 ounces sliced white mushrooms
2 celery stalks, diced
⅔ cup dried cranberries
⅔ cup roughly chopped hazelnuts
6 ounces cubed stuffing mix (about half a bag; 3 to 4 cups)
3 garlic cloves, grated or minced
⅔ cup dry white wine
½ cup milk
2 cups chicken stock
1 red apple, cored and sliced

Preheat the oven to 400°F. Adjust the rack to the middle position.

In a large, ovenproof skillet set over medium-high heat, combine about 2 teaspoons of the oil and the sausage. Brown the meat, breaking it up into crumbles as it cooks for about 4 minutes. Transfer to a paper towel–lined plate or tray and set aside.

Season the chicken thighs with salt, pepper, and the poultry seasoning (if the seasoning has salt, go light on the salt).

Add the remaining 1 teaspoon of oil to the skillet (or more if needed), still set over medium-high, and cook the chicken, skin-side down, until deeply browned, 3 to 4 minutes. Flip and cook for another 1 minute on the other side. Transfer to a plate and set aside.

Reduce the heat under the skillet to medium and combine the diced onion, bell pepper, mushrooms, celery, cranberries, and hazelnuts. If you need a little more oil, that's fine, too. Season everything lightly with salt and pepper. Cook, stirring occasionally, until the veggies are tender, 5 to 6 minutes. Add the stuffing and garlic and cook for 1 minute more while stirring.

Add the wine and stir to mix it in and to scrape up any browned bits on the bottom of the skillet. Next, add the milk and the stock, stirring to incorporate. Add the sausage back in, stir to combine, and the top with the chicken. Place apple slices around the chicken and then roast for 25 to 28 minutes, or until the chicken is cooked through and nice and crispy-brown on top.

Fancy Winter Fruit Salad

Salads don't get much lovelier than this, what with its deep, rich jewel tones and the not-so-subtle showering of chocolate on top. This makes a fantastic addition to any holiday table, and it's great for the cook, too, as you can make it in advance and it sits well at room temperature for as long as you need it to. It's built on truly seasonal ingredients, which makes it very special. You can only get these fruits for a limited time, just around the fall/winter holiday season.

They're widely available and easy to get during that time—but only during that time. This creates a magical air of fancy to this platter of juicy gemstone-esque fruits. The finishing olive oil pools together with the balsamic glaze and the slowly melting chocolate, creating a very merry scene, indeed.

Makes 4 servings

2 Fuyu persimmons
3 blood oranges, peeled and sliced into rounds or divided into supremes or wedges
Seeds from 1 pomegranate
4 ounces dark chocolate, finely chopped
¼ cup store-bought balsamic glaze, or to taste
Good extra virgin olive oil, for drizzling
Flaky sea salt, for sprinkling (optional)

Preheat the oven to 400°F.

Put the persimmons on a baking sheet and roast them whole until they're essentially half-baked, about 15 minutes. We don't want them to fall apart, but this par-baking softens them and brings out their flavor and soft sweetness. When they're cool enough to handle, trim off the tops and slice them as thinly as possible (I use a mandoline).

Arrange the persimmon slices on a big platter and add the sliced or segmented blood oranges. Sprinkle the pomegranate seeds all over and drizzle with lots of sticky balsamic glaze. Scatter the chopped chocolate all over and finish with a drizzle of nice olive oil. Flaky sea salt to finish is a nice idea, but optional.

Note *If you can't find persimmons, thinly sliced pear or apple work beautifully as well.*

Two-Ingredient Squash and Caramelized Onion Soup

With only two core ingredients, this soup is pure magic. A luscious, velvety puree of my favorite of all the squashes—the kabocha— and sweet, mellow (mostly) caramelized onions. Thanks to the inherent creaminess and built-in texture of the squash, no actual cream is needed for this soup. It's just squash and onions, and it will knock your socks off. I don't count cooking oil and salt and pepper as ingredients, for the same reason I don't count pots, pans, and sharp knives. They're too essential to the whole process, every single time. Ahem, anyway. This soup! It's gorgeous served in shot glasses, as a small starter before a holiday meal, or in big, deep bowls, topped with anything you like.

Makes 4 to 6 servings

1 small kabocha squash
　　or 1 butternut squash
　　(2 to 2½ pounds)
2 tablespoons olive oil
3 medium sweet onions,
　　thinly sliced
1½ teaspoons salt, divided,
　　plus more to taste
2½ cups water, divided,
　　plus more as needed

Freshly ground black
　　pepper, to taste
Plain yogurt, chopped fresh
　　herbs (parsley, tarragon,
　　and dill are my favorites),
　　roasted kabocha seeds, and/
　　or a drizzle of maple syrup,
　　for serving (optional)

Preheat the oven to 375°F. Adjust the rack to the middle position.

Place the squash directly on the oven rack and allow it to cook for 45 minutes. This will make it so much easier to cut and peel (trust me, it's totally worth this step). Once it's cool enough to handle, cut and peel away the tough outer skin and slice in half. Remove the seeds and then cut the squash into 1-inch pieces.

Meanwhile, pour the oil into a large, deep pot set over medium heat. Add the sliced onions and 1 teaspoon of the salt and cook, stirring frequently, until the onions have softened tremendously and turned a medium-brown or blondish color, about 30 minutes. We're not fully going for it here—it's a lighter caramelization.

Next, add the squash into the pot with the onions along with ½ cup of the water and the remaining ½ teaspoon of salt. Stir and cook for a few minutes, sort of mashing and breaking up the squash as you go.

Add 1 cup of water and transfer the mixture to a blender (or you can use an immersion blender if you have one). Blend until totally creamy and smooth. Pour back into the pot.

Taste the mixture and add salt and pepper as needed. Add the remaining 1 cup of water and stir. Stir! Stir. I typically use close to 3 cups of water to get to my ideal consistency, but this part is really up to you. You're mostly aiming for a velvety pureed soup consistency (not thick baby food). The soup will

reduce and thicken the longer you keep it over the heat. Also, if you get it too thin or watery, just let it cook a little longer.

Serve as it is or with toppings of your choice, such as dollops of plain yogurt, chopped herbs, roasted kabocha seeds, and maple syrup.

SPOTLIGHT

To toast the seeds from your kabocha squash, rinse and dry them thoroughly. Arrange them in a single layer on a baking sheet and let them air dry for about 1 hour. Toss with a little olive oil, salt, and pepper and roast at 300°F for about 40 minutes, stirring once halfway through.

Warm Radicchio and Squash Salad with Brown-Buttered Dates

I'd initially planned to give you a healthy spin on pumpkin pie in this chapter, as it seemed obligatory. But to be totally honest . . . I'd rather eat plates of this salad than pumpkin pie. It's the textures and salty, sweet flavors for me—plus the colors aren't terrible, either. The name is a little deceiving, as there are really only two tablespoons of butter in the whole recipe. It's there to anchor the dressing and add a nuttiness that feels holiday-special to me. I think you can opt for either pomegranate seeds or chopped hazelnuts for the crunchy element here (hazelnuts and browned butter have huge crushes on each other), but if you want to use both—I say go for it. It is the holidays, after all.

Makes 4 servings

1 medium butternut squash, about 3 pounds
1 teaspoon plus 3 tablespoons olive oil, plus more as needed
Salt
Freshly ground black pepper
1 teaspoon garam masala or curry powder
½ head radicchio, leaves separated (alternatively, you could chop it)
2 tablespoons butter
6 to 8 pitted dates, roughly chopped
2 tablespoons balsamic vinegar
⅓ cup pomegranate seeds and/ or chopped toasted hazelnuts

Preheat the oven to 375°F.

Place the unpeeled squash directly onto the oven rack and roast for 40 minutes. Allow it to cool until you can handle it, and then peel it (if desired—I often don't). Halve it lengthwise, scoop out the seeds, and slice into ½-inch half-moons.

Pour 1 or 2 teaspoons of the oil into a large (preferably) nonstick skillet over medium heat. If your skillet isn't nonstick, a little more oil might be necessary. Add the squash, then season well with salt, pepper, and the garam masala. Cook the squash on both sides until browned and crusty, 6 to 8 minutes per side. They're already well on their way since we preroasted. So just get things nice, tender, and beautifully brown.

Arrange the radicchio on a large plate or tray (or individual plates) and top with the cooked squash. Add the butter to the skillet along with the dates. Allow the butter to melt and then brown, stirring occasionally—this will take about 5 minutes.

When you can smell the nuttiness of the browned butter, add 3 to 5 more tablespoons of oil (depending on your preference), the balsamic vinegar, and some salt and pepper to taste. Stir to mix and to get those dates crispy and caramelized. Spoon this warm vinaigrette over the squash and radicchio and top with the pomegranate seeds or chopped hazelnuts (or both!).

Milky Oven-Braised Carrots

I'm sort of pushing an agenda with this one, which is simply the fact that I want people to both embrace and explore the wonders of cooking with flavor pastes. It doesn't sound at all glamorous, but it's a simple trick that can level up your food in a hurry. Similar to my Southern Summer Concentrate (page 20) this recipe demonstrates the power that a small scoopful of a very concentrated flavor blend can wield. Southern cooks know how to make vegetables sing with flavor, and here, I'm basically giving you one of my very best vegetable-singing tricks. We'll scorch and then braise the heck out of the veggie in question (here, the carrot), all the while imbuing them with intense, aromatic flavors from helpful pals like garlic, anchovy, and herbs.

Makes 4 to 6 servings

16 ounces fresh whole carrots (they're typically sold in this quantity)
2 tablespoons olive oil
3 anchovies, finely chopped
1 tablespoon grated fresh ginger
1 tablespoon stock concentrate (either chicken, vegetable, or Southern Summer Concentrate, page 20)
3 garlic cloves, grated
1 (15-ounce) can coconut milk
Salt
½ cup peanuts, pecans, or pistachios, chopped
½ cup chopped fresh mint
½ cup chopped fresh cilantro

Preheat the oven to 400°F. Adjust the rack to the middle position.

If your carrots have leafy tops, trim those off and discard or set aside for another use. No need to peel! Pour the oil into a large pan over medium-high heat. When it's hot, add the carrots and sear them madly, turning occasionally, until black splotches form and they look nice and charred. This takes 5 minutes or so.

Transfer the carrots to a roasting or baking dish, leaving the oil in the pan.

Reduce the heat to low and, in the same pan, add the anchovies, ginger, stock concentrate, and grated garlic. Cook for about 1 minute and then add the coconut milk. Season lightly with salt and then pour it over the carrots. Place in the oven and braise until the carrots are very tender and the coconut milk is caramelized, about 25 minutes.

Top with the chopped nuts, mint, and cilantro before serving.

A Green Bean Un-Casserole for Mushroom Lovers

This is my reimagined take on a vintage green bean casserole, but I've broken the classic down somewhat and am playing around with each part. I have always been especially interested in the mushroom aspect of green bean casseroles. I think this is largely due to the fact that they're nowhere near as good as they could be—a sad, wasted flavor opportunity. There are cans to blame for this. My recipe here kicks the cans (ha!) to the curb and leans way into roasted fresh green beans and the umami-bombs that are dried porcini mushrooms. I'm really driving home the whole fungi component of the program for you, fellow die hard mushroom lovers. This un-casserole's for you.

Makes 4 servings

1 ½ pounds fresh green beans, trimmed
2 tablespoons plus 2 teaspoons olive oil, divided, plus more as needed
½ teaspoon salt, plus more
Freshly ground black pepper
4 shallots, very thinly sliced (I use a mandoline)
½ cup cottage cheese
½ ounce dried porcini mushrooms (typically sold in 1-ounce packages)
½ teaspoon nutritional yeast
1 garlic clove
½ cup buttermilk or whole milk
1 lemon, zested and quartered

Preheat the oven to 425°F.

Put the green beans on a baking sheet, drizzle with 2 teaspoons of the oil, and season lightly with salt and pepper. Roast for 25 to 30 minutes, or until charred and tender.

Meanwhile, pour the remaining 2 tablespoons of oil into a large (preferably) nonstick skillet over medium heat. When it's hot, add the sliced shallots, season lightly with salt and pepper, and let them cook 10 to 12 minutes, stirring occasionally, until very deeply brown. Transfer to a plate and set aside.

Meanwhile, in a food processor, combine the cottage cheese, dried porcinis, nutritional yeast, ½ teaspoon of salt, the garlic, and buttermilk. Process until smooth. Taste and adjust the seasonings to your liking. Spread this creamy mixture on the bottom of a large serving platter. It makes a lot, so just use however much you like, and save the rest.

Pile the roasted green beans on top of the porcini cream and scatter the frizzled shallots over top. Sprinkle the lemon zest over top. Serve the lemon quarters alongside the beans, for squeezing, if desired.

SPOTLIGHT

The shallots won't crisp up as well for you if they're cooking on top of each other, so a large skillet is key here. Also, quality nonstick cookware reduces the amount of oil or cooking fat necessary—a true asset in lighter cooking.

Caramelized Sweet Potatoes with Vanilla Cream and Hot Honey

The classic Southern-style sweet potato casserole cleans up pretty nice, it turns out. In a "what's not to love" sort of way, I actually do enjoy the sugar, marshmallow, and butter-bedecked iteration that rents space on so many Southern holiday tables. But I am in full-blown love with this version. Sweet potatoes caramelize brilliantly on their own, needing no help from added sugar. And I've laced my favorite yogurty whipped cream with lots of vanilla to give it a boost of luscious sweetness, befitting any holiday or special occasion table. Hot honey is available just about everywhere now, and when you combine it with the smoky almonds—you've got what just might be my favorite recipe in the whole book.

Makes up to 8 servings

4 sweet potatoes, halved lengthwise
3 teaspoons olive oil, plus extra for coating
Kosher salt
Freshly ground black pepper
1 cup heavy whipping cream
1 cup vanilla Greek or regular yogurt
1 teaspoon vanilla bean paste or the seeds of 1 vanilla bean (optional)
Store-bought hot honey, for drizzling
¼ cup finely chopped smoked almonds
Flaky sea salt, for topping (optional)

Preheat the oven to 425°F and adjust the rack to the middle position. Line a large baking sheet with parchment paper.

Coat each sweet potato half with oil and season generously with salt and pepper. Place them on the baking sheet cut-sides down and roast until fork-tender, about 45 minutes.

Pour 3 teaspoons of the oil into a large nonstick skillet set over medium-high heat. When it's hot, sear the sweet potatoes, cut-sides down, until nicely browned and deeply caramelized, about 3 minutes. Transfer to a platter or individual plates.

In a stand mixer or in a mixing bowl using a hand-held mixer, whip the heavy cream until stiff peaks form. Add the vanilla yogurt and, if using, vanilla paste. Whip just to evenly combine and spoon down around and/or on top of the sweet potatoes. Drizzle with hot honey, sprinkle with smoked almonds, and if you like a little extra salt—a sprinkle of flaky sea salt is nice here. Serve warm.

The Joys of a Simple Roasted Vegetable Platter

This is another entry that is much more idea than recipe. I will, however, supply you with ingredient amounts and cook times that are meant to be used loosely, as simple guidelines that you may absolutely step over (and even totally disregard) as you like. Here's the deal: I think crudité platters are just okay—"delish-ish" as my husband says. They're fine in a pinch, but by simply giving our raw veggies a good, hard roast in some fruity olive oil with lots of salt and pepper, you've taken the most classic (and boring!) party appetizer and catapulted it to a much more delicious place. This is a great healthy grazing option at large and small gatherings alike. Just set out a big platter heaped with your roasted veggies, with some small plates and toothpicks and/or adorable tiny forks alongside, and watch people devour them (they will!). Simply put, roasted vegetables > not-roasted vegetables.

Some nice things to keep in mind: You can use any veggies that you like, really. This list just reflects what I tend to do, because it makes for an attractive, colorful mix and each item here is typically sold in the amount or quantity given, so there's no waste. But broccoli and cauliflower would be great, and so would mushrooms! See also: Brussels sprouts, cherry tomatoes . . . you get the idea.

Everything roasts at 425°F, and most things cook in pretty much the same amount of time, give or take 10 minutes. Sturdier, denser veggies (like carrots and potatoes) take a little longer, as you might imagine. Just take each vegetable out of the oven when it looks great to you—a little charred and visibly tender. That's as fussy as this recipe gets. Throw everything on a big platter as they're done roasting, and enjoy the fact that all of these things taste just as good hot as they do at room temperature. I use two or three large baking sheets, depending on how many veggies I'm roasting. The key is to make sure each vegetable gets its own area on the pan, so you can easily transfer them to your serving platter when they finish cooking (i.e., don't toss/mix them up). Parchment paper will be your best friend here, so far as the post-roast cleanup goes. Trust me.

Makes 6 to 8 servings as an appetizer

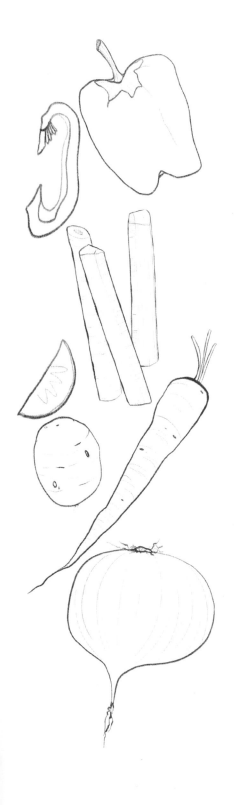

16 ounces baby carrots (or 3 large carrots, cut into bite-size pieces)

1 red onion, cut into 1-inch petals

1 zucchini, sliced into ¼-inch rounds

1 yellow squash, sliced into ¼-inch rounds

24 ounces baby yellow potatoes, halved

3 bell peppers, mixed colors, sliced

Olive oil, for drizzling

Salt

Freshly ground black pepper

Comeback Sauce (page 22)

Scorned-Women Hot Sauce (page 24)

Herby, Lemony Yogurt (page 21)

Pimiento Cheese Hummus (page 119)

Preheat the oven to 425°F. Adjust 1 rack to the top position and 1 in the lower position.

Line 2 or 3 baking sheets or roasting pans with parchment paper and divide the vegetables up among them, keeping each veggie type separate. Drizzle everything with the oil and season generously with salt and pepper. Toss to coat, still keeping each type separate.

Roast the vegetables until they're visibly tender and lightly browned or charred. The potatoes and carrots will take more like 35 to 40 minutes, and softer things like zucchini and bell peppers are done in 25 to 30 minutes. Toss everything halfway through. As they finish, pile each veggie up on a big platter in their own section, and serve with any sauces or dipping elements you like.

SWEET LIGHTS

The line wraps around an entire city block.
Sweet breezes put everyone under a
just-baked, sugar-spun spell.

It's a sweet trip to the candy shoppe . . .

Breaths fogging up window panes,
little noses pressed against glass,
they hope for a glimpse of the bakery's magic.

Kids and grown-ups alike
delight in the simple fact of
their immediate futures.

For just around the corner awaits
fluffy buttercream, sticky-sweet
gumdrops, sparkling fruit towers,
sky-high pies, fluffy muffins, and
chocolate-covered everything.

Sugar, spice, and everything nice.

These precious sweet things add
so much shine to our days.

The from-scratch, blink-and-you'll-miss-them,
freshly-baked-with-love things.

The delicious, fleeting moments
that are always worth the wait.

Jammy Kiwi-Berry Pandowdy

This juicy old-fashioned confection occupies the same space as the cobblers, pies, crisps, crumbles, buckles, and Bettys of the baking world. I love this world, and I spend a lot of time there in my recipe daydreaming. Simple and straightforward, pandowdies are like pies with messy, haphazard "dowdied" crusts. No lattices, braids, crimping, or special cutting required. How refreshing, right? They're truly the best for that reason alone. Also, unlike most classic fruit pies, we're using only one crust here, not two. This pandowdy allows us to indulge in a classic buttery pie crust, while automatically halving the amount we consume in each serving. It's small shifts like these that really add up over time. Also, I think we should be baking with kiwis more—they are among the most nutritious foods out there and work beautifully in cozy bakes like this one.

Makes 6 to 8 servings

Natural nonstick cooking spray
4 cups mixed berries (about 2 pounds), fresh or thawed frozen, halved if large
2 cups sliced kiwi (5 or 6 kiwi)
½ cup maple syrup
2 teaspoons coconut sugar
¼ teaspoon salt
2 teaspoons vanilla bean paste or extract
3½ tablespoons cornstarch
1 pie crust (either your favorite homemade or store-bought and thawed is fine)
Buttermilk or whole milk, for brushing
Turbinado sugar, for sprinkling
Vanilla frozen yogurt, for serving

Preheat the oven to 375°F. Adjust the oven rack to the middle position.

In a large cast-iron skillet or baking dish that has been sprayed with cooking spray, combine the berries and kiwi. Add the maple syrup, coconut sugar, salt, vanilla, and cornstarch. Toss until well mixed.

Place the pie dough on a clean, floured work surface and roll it out (in whatever shape is most appropriate) until it is large enough to cover the pan (see Note). Lay the crust over the filling in the skillet and tuck or trim the edges to fit as needed. Brush with buttermilk, sprinkle with turbinado sugar, and bake for 25 minutes.

Pull the skillet out of the oven and, using a knife, cut and stab the parbaked crust to bust and break it up into pieces. We're dowdy-ing it! (This releases air and lets the juices bubble up and caramelize. It is also cathartic.)

Bake for 30 to 35 minutes more, or until the crust pieces are very golden brown and cooked through. Let it rest for at least 10 minutes before serving with vanilla frozen yogurt.

Note *You can also break or cut up the raw pie crust and lay those pieces all over the top of the fruit in the pan before baking. Just skip the whole stabbing part—no need. Works just as well.*

Apples with Smoked Almonds and Tahini, Cardamom, and Date Caramel

Sometimes dessert needs to be nothing more than really great fruit and something special to highlight it. This recipe embraces the solid notion of "dips for dessert," a concept on which fondue has really cornered the market. I suppose it also tips its hat to the caramel apple—which is the greatest dessert moment of the whole year, in my opinion. My affection for the aforementioned things led me to this—this totally plant-based version that is a weird-but-delicious little mix of characters. We'll (literally) whip up a much lighter take on caramel sauce, by way of a delicious date caramel. The small bit of tahini and cardamom are there because they're two of my favorite things and I wanted to include them in this apple party.

Makes 4 to 6 servings, as a snack or appetizer

2 apples, cored and sliced (Honeycrisp if you can)

⅓ cup finely chopped smoked almonds (or as much as you like!)

1 batch Tahini, Cardamom, and Date Caramel (page 22)

Arrange the sliced apples on a platter and cover with the smoked almond bits. Serve with the caramel sauce.

Boozy Bananas Foster Bread Pudding

Imagine the happiest marriage between banana bread, Southern-style bread pudding, and classic Bananas Foster … that's what I'm aiming for with this recipe, and it's a union over which I'm happy to preside. In my lighter take on not one but three classic Southern treats, I'm replacing nearly half of the bread in my go-to bread pudding recipe with bananas and even blending a fresh banana into the custard. This is great served with vanilla frozen yogurt, Yogurty Whipped Cream (page 21), or (if you're me) a thick slather of Tahini, Cardamom, and Date Caramel (page 22), which sits atop this pudding like a thick layer of miraculously healthy frosting.

Makes at least 8 servings

Note *If the pudding starts to look too brown on top before it's cooked through, just lay a sheet of aluminum foil over top until it has finished baking.*

2 cups low-fat milk or vanilla almond milk
18 pitted dates
2 tablespoons spiced rum or bourbon
4 ripe bananas, divided
6 large eggs
2 teaspoons vanilla extract
½ teaspoon ground cinnamon
1 tablespoon molasses

Natural nonstick cooking spray
12 Hawaiian sweet rolls, quartered
Turbinado sugar, for sprinkling
Tahini, Cardamom, and Date Caramel (page 22), for serving
Vanilla frozen yogurt, for serving

In a medium saucepan set over medium heat, combine the milk, dates, and rum. Let it come to a simmer and then turn off the heat. Let the dates soak and soften for 10 minutes. Pour the mixture into a high-speed blender and add 1 banana and the eggs, vanilla, cinnamon, and molasses. Blend until totally smooth.

Spray a 9 x 13-inch baking pan with cooking spray (or you can bake this in a large soufflé dish or even individual ramekins; your bake time will just vary).

Thinly slice the remaining 3 bananas. Arrange the Hawaiian roll pieces and the sliced banana in the prepared baking dish. Pour the boozy custard over top and push everything down to fully submerge. Let the custard soak into the bread and bananas for at least 1 hour.

To bake, preheat the oven to 350°F. Adjust the rack to the middle position.

Sprinkle the pudding with a generous coating of turbinado sugar. Bake the bread pudding until it is deeply browned on top and set in the center (not visibly wet or jiggly), 45 to 50 minutes. If you're baking in a soufflé dish, it could be more like 65 to 75 minutes, just FYI. Using small ramekins? You're looking at 30 to 40 minutes.

Your pudding will likely sink a little as it cools—this is totally normal! You can fill the caverns in with date caramel, which is what I like to do. Serve with vanilla frozen yogurt and another swirl of caramel.

Ruffled Buttermilk (Punch) Pie

The halls of classic Southern confectionery are decked with luscious, rich, sugary-sweet pies. Not a moment goes by where there isn't a warm pie cooling on a windowsill somewhere. From chess, coconut cream, and pecan to the transparent and Derby pies from my home state of Kentucky, almost every nook and cranny of the Southland is fit to burst with examples of beloved regional pies. My favorite of them all is a simple buttermilk pie, and I've long used the recipe from Lisa Donovan, the James Beard Award–winning pastry chef, food writer, and fearless leader of Nashville's former Buttermilk Road pop-up dinner series. My recipe here honors hers and my love of a simple, un-frilled Southern pie.

Makes 1 (9-inch) pie

Natural nonstick cooking spray
10 sheets frozen phyllo dough, thawed
5 large eggs, beaten
1½ cups buttermilk
⅓ cup maple syrup
2 tablespoons honey
1 ounce bourbon or spiced rum (optional)
½ teaspoon ground cinnamon
3 teaspoons vanilla extract or vanilla bean paste
¼ teaspoon freshly grated nutmeg
Turbinado sugar, for sprinkling
Fresh berries, powdered sugar, toasted almonds, and/or Yogurty Whipped Cream (page 21), for topping

Preheat the oven to 350°F. Adjust the rack to the middle position. Spray a 9-inch springform pan or 9-inch cake pan with cooking spray and line with parchment paper, ensuring there is ample overhang so you can easily remove the pie after it cools (think of the overhang as your handles). Put the pan on a baking sheet.

Scrunch up the sheets of phyllo and haphazardly arrange them in the prepared pan. Just push and squeeze them in, covering the surface of the pan. There is no need for precision or perfection here, as that is not at all the point. The more jagged, jutting points and edges sticking out, the better.

In a mixing bowl, whisk together the eggs, buttermilk, maple syrup, honey, bourbon (if using), cinnamon, and vanilla. Pour this over the phyllo in the pan. Sprinkle the fresh nutmeg over top.

Bake the pie until very golden and set, about 40 minutes. Sprinkle generously with turbinado sugar right when it comes out of the oven, evenly covering the surface. Let it cool for 10 minutes before transferring it elsewhere and top with fresh berries, toasted almonds, and/or whipped cream.

Peanut Butter-Sesame Cookie Brittle

Nutty and almost smoky-sweet, this is like a happy cross between a peanut butter cookie and peanut brittle. It's got a chewy crunch—a texture all its own, to be honest, that I find downright irresistible. The small bit of toasted sesame oil is really what keeps things interesting here, deepening the flavor and giving it a sort of grown-up feel. In a nod to Charleston's beloved benne seed (like an heirloom sesame seed), I've added sesame seeds to this as well. They add a nice texture to this candy shoppe-esque treat. Maple syrup and coconut sugar work together beautifully—no refined sugar needed. This stuff never lasts more than a day in my house.

Makes 8 to 10 servings

1 cup coconut sugar
¼ cup maple syrup
¼ cup water
⅔ cup roasted peanuts
1 tablespoon benne seeds (or toasted sesame seeds)
2 tablespoons creamy natural peanut butter
½ teaspoon toasted sesame oil
½ teaspoon baking soda
Flaky sea salt, for sprinkling

Line a large baking sheet with parchment paper or a silicone baking mat.

In a heavy-bottom pot set over medium heat (no higher!), bring the coconut sugar, maple syrup, and water to a simmer. Add the peanuts and benne seeds, and stir just to combine.

Cook, with no more stirring, until just before the mixture reaches 300°F. This can take anywhere from 5 to 20 minutes, so just be patient. It will get there, and it might even smell almost burnt at the very end. Have faith! It's okay.

As soon as the mixture hits 300°F, take it off the heat and stir in the peanut butter, sesame oil, and baking soda. Stir to combine and immediately pour the brittle mixture onto the prepared baking sheet, covering as much surface area of the sheet as you can. It should naturally spread on its own. Counterintuitively, trying to smooth it out will actually do the opposite. Just let it spread and fall where it will. The thinner the better, though.

Sprinkle with a good pinch of flaky sea salt, and let your cookie-brittle cool and firm up on the baking sheet until it easily breaks apart into smaller pieces, about 30 minutes. This will keep in a covered container in a cool dry place for up to 5 days.

Vegan Preacher Cookies

Legend has it that this name is derived from the sweet treats Southern housewives would whip up at a moment's notice when visited unexpectedly by their local preachers. This tracks, as these cookies are very fast and easy to prepare, and they also happen to take me right back to my childhood.

The chocolatey, peanut-buttery flavor and crunchy oat texture is so familiar—deliciously nostalgic with every bite. These are a version of "icebox cookies" in that they should be stored in either the refrigerator or freezer. The chocolate and coconut oil blend will melt in both your mouth and your hands, and is best when chilled.

I love this combination of flavors and textures so much; I even use it as the base for icebox pies and cakes.

Makes about 12 cookies

½ cup creamy natural peanut butter
¼ cup maple syrup
½ teaspoon salt
¼ cup solid coconut oil
2 teaspoons vanilla extract
2 tablespoons unsweetened cocoa powder
1 ½ cups quick-cooking oats

Line a baking sheet with parchment paper or a silicone baking mat.

In a saucepan set over medium heat, stir together the peanut butter, maple syrup, salt, and coconut oil. Keep stirring until everything is fully melted and well mixed.

Stir in the vanilla and cocoa powder. Add the oats and mix to combine.

Drop the mixture in tablespoons onto the prepared baking sheet, allowing the cookies to set up in the refrigerator for a few hours. Store in a covered container in either the refrigerator or freezer. These work best when served cold—even frozen—as the heat from our hands causes the ingredients to slowly melt. The colder the better!

Snow Cream for Southerners

Snowfall in Charleston is discussed in much the same way as solar eclipses and blue moons—a rarity to be sure. Many corners of the South don't see much action in the wintry weather department, so this recipe is my playful solution should one ever find themself pining for it. This couldn't be simpler, and it's best when personalized to one's preferences, like a sundae bar. For me to tell you how to flavor your snow cream would be like me telling you how to get dressed in the morning— it's not my place. Do you like honey more than maple syrup? Use that as your sweetener. Vanilla is always good, and so is coconut cream.

Good on a hot summer's day or in the dead of winter when the snow just won't fall, this homespun take on fresh snow cream is guaranteed to make anyone smile.

Makes about 2 servings

6 cups of ice cubes (amount is approximate)

FLAVORINGS (AMOUNTS VARY DEPENDING ON PERSONAL PREFERENCE)

Coconut cream (shake the can before opening it)
Coconut sugar
Maple syrup
Honey

Vanilla extract
Turbinado sugar, for sparkling snow
Naturally colored rainbow sprinkles

Fill a high-speed blender halfway with ice cubes and process on the "ice crush" setting until the ice is completely crushed and has a very "snow-like" consistency. You could also do this in a food processor, if needed. Quickly transfer the "snow" to a large mixing bowl, or divide among individual bowls, as you like.

Stir in a little bit of coconut cream to add richness and creaminess, and then add any of the suggested flavorings and/ or toppings.

Bursting-Berry Company Cake

This is a health-ified version of one of the most popular recipes I have ever shared, and dare I say I think I prefer this one? I have become a true devotee of coconut sugar, and swapping in white whole wheat flour is always an easy move—one that does just a little more for you. With its simple lineup of everyday baking standards, this cake is so laid back—perfect for having people over or transporting elsewhere (hence the name). Have cake, will travel! I love the vibrant berry bursts all over the cake, and I'm just a sucker for a crumbly, streusel-y topping. Always and forever.

Makes 1 (10-inch) cake

FOR THE CAKE
Natural nonstick cooking spray
1 ½ cups white whole wheat flour
2 teaspoons baking powder
Scant 1 teaspoon baking soda
¾ cup brown coconut sugar
½ teaspoon salt
⅔ cup melted coconut oil (see Note)
⅔ cup buttermilk
2 large eggs, beaten
2 teaspoons vanilla extract
2 ½ cups fresh or frozen mixed berries

FOR THE CRUMBLE TOPPING
½ cup white whole wheat flour
⅓ cup brown coconut sugar
3 tablespoons solid coconut oil

To make the cake: Preheat the oven to 350°F. Spray a 10-inch springform pan with cooking spray.

In a large bowl, mix together the flour, baking powder, baking soda, coconut sugar, and salt. To this mixture, add the coconut oil, buttermilk, eggs, and vanilla. Stir just until everything is well blended.

Pour the batter into the prepared pan. Top with the berries.

To make the crumble topping: In a medium bowl, combine the flour, coconut sugar, and solid coconut oil. Using your fingers (I think this just works best), mix and mash the ingredients together until a crumbly streusel forms. Sprinkle this streusel over the berries in the pan.

Bake the cake for 40 to 45 minutes, or until lightly golden brown on top and set. Allow the cake to cool almost all the way before removing it from the pan.

> **Note** *Coconut oil is typically sold in a solid form, which we'll use for the crumble topping here. But for the batter, we need it to be liquefied, which is easily accomplished by simply microwaving briefly (like butter). Alternatively, coconut oil can be melted in a small saucepan on the stovetop.*

The Healthy Southern Soda Fountain

Bubbly, sweet, and infinite when it comes to their flavor possibilities, these simple homemade drinks are such a fun way to enjoy sodas without all of the sugar and/or questionable additives contained within so many store-bought varieties. These sodas are built on an easy juice plus honey simple syrup, whose flavor really just depends on the juice you use. My kids love strawberry-banana and mixed berry, but I am partial to cranberry and orange-vanilla. As long as you opt for 100 percent juice (no added sugar) you're well on your way to a much more healthful soda option.

Makes 4 (12-ounce) sodas

1 cup 100 percent juice (any flavor you like)
½ cup honey
1 tablespoon juice-sweetened all-fruit spread (any flavor you like)
1 teaspoon vanilla extract (optional)

48 ounces lemon-lime seltzer water (or unflavored)
12-ounce clear glass bottles with tops, or something comparable (easily purchased online)

In a small saucepan over medium heat, combine the juice, honey, and fruit spread. Let it come to a gentle simmer and stir to melt the honey and fruit spread into the juice. Simmer the syrup for 10 minutes, turn off the heat, and add the vanilla (if using). Let the syrup cool completely before transferring to a lidded storage container. The syrup will keep in the refrigerator for about 1 week.

TO MAKE A SODA

Pour your desired amount of honey-fruit syrup into each bottle (I typically use ¼ to ⅓ cup per drink). Top with the seltzer. Refrigerate before enjoying, and be sure to gently turn the bottles over a few times (don't shake!) to mix the syrup into the seltzer before drinking, as it will settle.

EPILOGUE

en·light·ened /in'lītnd, en'lītnd/ adjective
having or showing a rational, modern, and well-informed outlook

A CONFESSION: This book was meant to open with a healthy biscuit recipe. And this was not just any biscuit recipe, mind you. It was an Avocado and Olive Oil Biscuit. I wish I could see your face as you read that just now, I really do.

I tested, reworked, outsourced, and really pushed hard for these things. My kitchen was covered in a fine patina of very healthy and wholesome flours for weeks because of this. But then it hit me. Boom! An enlightenment.

Biscuits, it turns out, are really and truly not meant for lightening, and now I know this to be true. You see, reader, when a classic buttermilk biscuit is trifled with, things happen and people get sad. If you have to force it—if you have to work this hard at it—it's probably best to just leave it alone and walk away.

Many recipes lighten up beautifully, with no cost to their deliciousness. But a biscuit? Not so much.

They were glaringly, and dare I say, offensively worse when I tried to weave in more wholesome, lighter ingredients.

After more attempts than I care to share, it became clear to me that it wasn't meant to be. I simply could not force some half-hearted light biscuit into this book just because I wanted it to be here.

So I backed off and backed away from the healthy oils and fats, the avocado and whole wheat flour. Instead, I grabbed my best grass-fed salted butter and full-fat buttermilk. I pulled my bag of White Lily flour off the shelf and made a batch of my favorite classic, extremely buttery buttermilk biscuits. Their salty, crunchy tops and tender insides are one of life's great, simple joys.

And who am I to mess with that?

Consider this biscuit recipe as a symbol of sorts, representing the final component of that philosophy: the importance of the occasional indulgence.

We need to walk away from the rules every now and again in order to follow them for the long run. So I say go ahead and "cheat" a little bit. If we never do this, how could we possibly uphold the lighter cooking way of life—how would we sustain it? Seems unrealistic to me.

And with that, we biscuit.

An Enlightened Buttermilk Biscuit

Here she is, my favorite ultra-buttery buttermilk biscuit. Every single aspect of this recipe is here for a reason and arrived at a different time and place from the others. The butter I use, the specific combination of flours, the temperature of the oven, the salt—all of it has gradually fallen into place over many years of happy biscuiteering.

I have whipped up and tinkered around with this recipe so much over so many years that it feels like coming home every time I set out to make them. It's the way the house smells. It's the sight of them cooling in the pan. It's accepting the utterly fleeting nature of their brief existence. These are blink-and-you'll-miss-them biscuits, usually vanishing before they've even had time to cool.

Makes 8 biscuits

1 ½ cups all-purpose flour
1 ½ cups cake flour, plus extra for flouring
1 tablespoon plus 1 teaspoon baking powder
¼ teaspoon baking soda
1 ½ teaspoons kosher salt
1 cup (2 sticks) salted butter, cut into pea-size bits (good quality, grass-fed if you can)
1 cup full-fat buttermilk, plus extra for brushing
Flaky sea salt, for sprinkling

In a large mixing bowl, combine the all-purpose flour, cake flour, baking powder, baking soda, and kosher salt. Whisk thoroughly to combine.

Using a pastry blender or (even better) your hands, work the butter into the dry mixture until you have a shaggy, even, well-blended dough. Add the buttermilk and stir or mix to bring it together into a cohesive dough.

Transfer the dough to a floured work surface and pat it into a 1-inch-tall circle. Using a large knife, cut the circle in half and stack 1 half on top of the other. Press down until you have a ¾-inch-tall circle. From this, cut your biscuits. You can use a knife and just cut them that way or use a cutter—up to you! I use a 1 ½-inch round cutter.

Arrange the biscuits on a baking sheet or in a cast-iron skillet so that all of their sides are touching (they will climb up and support each other as they rise). Brush with a little buttermilk and sprinkle lightly with sea salt. Put the biscuits in the fridge while the oven preheats.

Preheat the oven to 425°F. Adjust the rack to the middle position.

Bake the biscuits until deeply golden on top and cooked through, 35 to 40 minutes.

ACKNOWLEDGMENTS

THIS BOOK WAS A TRUE JOY TO MAKE. I loved all the nooks and crannies of it—from creating the concept and fleshing it all out to the recipe development, testing (and retesting!), shooting and styling, and the editing of it all. I'm thrilled to see it get its wings and fly out into the world, absolutely. But there is a part of me that is a little sad to see it go. The fun, as they say, is in the journey, and making books has been a real testament to the veracity of that notion. The people I met and with whom I worked throughout the whole process—from the very beginning all the way to end—are what really made it fun. This book is so much cooler than it would have been without the helping hands of so many generous, talented, supportive souls. So to them I owe a big fat debt of gratitude. I'm so very thankful.

To my family, first and foremost—thank you again and again for your patience and the copious amounts of grace you gave to me as I worked on this book. It was . . . a lot. Lucas, Elle, and Easton—you three are my heart.

To my agent, Deborah Ritchken, without whom there would be no books at all—I remain very thankful that I found you all those years ago. Thank you for faithfully shepherding my ideas into the homes of best fit.

To my recipe testers—you incredible collective of wonderful cooks! I was, am, and will always be so amazed at your willingness to try all sorts of recipes. To Rosa Jankowski and Madison Russell in particular, your generosity and supportive spirits are gifts. Thank you so much.

To Tiffany—as a longtime fan of your work, I'm so incredibly honored to have your illustrations in this book. What I didn't expect when I asked, in my very dorky, very "check yes or no" sort of way, was that I'd get to call you a friend, too. I'm grateful to Beth, who showed off your magic and led me to you.

To my editor, Michelle Branson, and the team at Gibbs Smith—thank you for giving my fledgling seed of a book a real home, a perfect garden in which to do all of its growing. I'm not what one would call a "details person," so having a team of people who are in fact, just that, is really amazing and I'm so happy to have had the chance to work with you.

And lastly, to my MKL readers (and my former Harvest and Honey readers)—thank you for hanging out with me all these years. This book wouldn't exist without you, so yeah, you could say I'm thankful.

INDEX

Metric Conversion Chart

Volume Measurements		Weight Measurements		Temperature	
U.S.	Metric	U.S.	Metric	Fahrenheit	Celsius
1 teaspoon	5 ml	½ ounce	15 g	250	120
1 tablespoon	15 ml	1 ounce	30 g	300	150
¼ cup	60 ml	3 ounces	80 g	325	160
⅓ cup	80 ml	4 ounces	115 g	350	175
½ cup	125 ml	8 ounces	225 g	375	190
⅔ cup	160 ml	12 ounces	340 g	400	200
¾ cup	180 ml	1 pound	450 g	425	220
1 cup	250 ml	2 ¼ pounds	1 kg	450	230

LAUREN McDUFFIE is a cookbook author (*Smoke, Roots, Mountain, Harvest*), food blogger, photographer/stylist, and creator of the cooking blog, My Kitchen Little. She is also the creator of the critically acclaimed and award-winning food blog, Harvest and Honey, and has articles, recipes, and photography published in various forms. Originally from Lexington, Kentucky, Lauren now lives in Charleston, South Carolina, with her husband and two children.

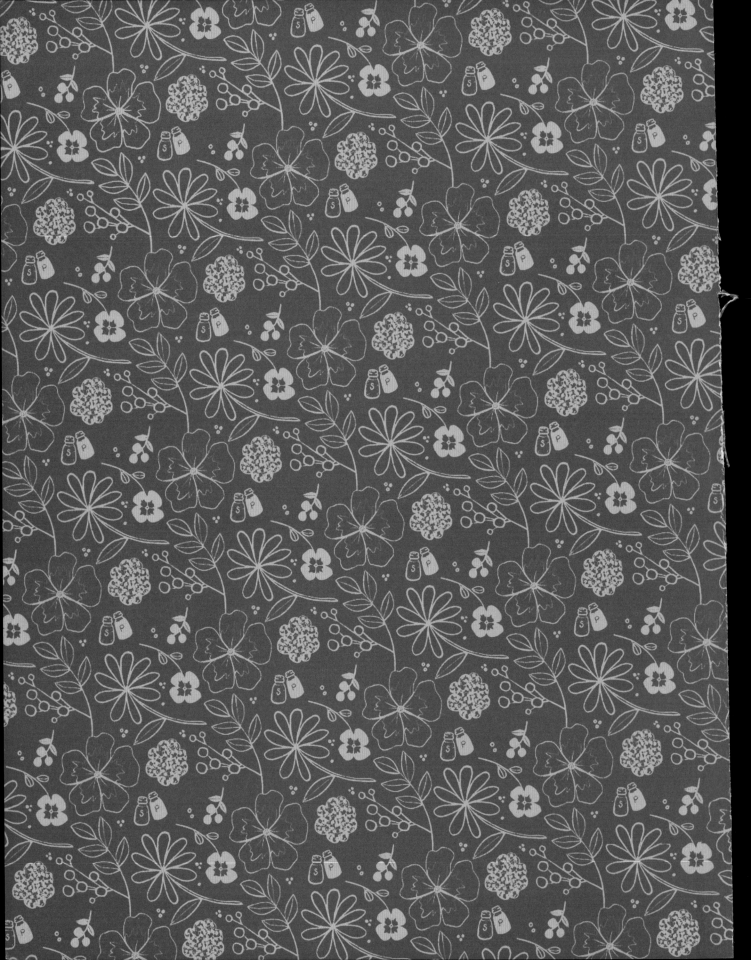